STREET
E&E

STREET

E&E

Evading, Escaping, and Other Ways to Save Your Ass When Things Get Ugly

Marc "Animal" MacYoung

PALADIN PRESS
BOULDER, COLORADO

Also by Marc "Animal" MacYoung:

Cheap Shots, Ambushes, and Other Lessons:
A Down and Dirty Book on Streetfighting and Survival

Fists, Wits, and a Wicked Right:
Surviving on the Wild Side of the Street

Floor Fighting: Stompings, Maimings, and Other Things
to Avoid When a Fight Goes to the Floor

Knives, Knife Fighting, and Related Hassles:
How to Survive a *Real* Knife Fight

Pool Cues, Beer Bottles, & Baseball Bats:
Animal's Guide to Improvised Weapons
for Self-Defense and Survival

Violence, Blunders, and Fractured Jaws:
Advanced Awareness Techniques and Street Etiquette

Street E & E:
Evading, Escaping, and Other Ways to Save Your Ass
When Things Get Ugly
by Marc "Animal" MacYoung

Copyright © 1993 by Marc "Animal" MacYoung

ISBN 0-87364-743-2
Printed in the United States of America

Published by Paladin Press, a division of
Paladin Enterprises, Inc., P.O. Box 1307,
Boulder, Colorado 80306, USA.
(303) 443-7250

Direct inquiries and/or orders to the above address.

Contents

Preface

One thing that used to piss me off about martial arts books is they don't tell you everything you need to know. They either assume you know the basics, or they want you to sign up with them in their particular system. They tell you all sorts of stuff that you didn't want to know and don't give you the stuff that you're hungry for. The other thing I've always suspected is that they're pitching extraneous information so they make money off you while you flounder through the morass of excessive information.

It never was my intent to write so many books on the subject of street violence. My original plan was to write a small booklet to get out of having to repeat myself to my students. The next thing I knew, I was hooked writing a book about everything I had wanted to know when I was coming up through the streets. Everything that would have made my life easier I tried to put into the first book. It didn't work; instead of getting it off my chest, I opened a huge can of worms.

Since that time, I've been writing specialized books for different aspects of this violent world. Unless you're a hard-core scrapper, I don't recommend that you read everything I've ever written. However, I find that as I go along I'm referring back to previous works more and more. To me it's all part of the bigger picture, but I figure most people don't want to spend their lives like I did and truly study the arts of war. To help you find the information you need, I've created a road map for some of the terms that I used in this book. It's a guide to which books and videos explain the concepts that I mention.

Also, I've included what I consider to be networks of books and videos that I think go together for a particular result. For example, if you want to know about knife fighting, my book about street etiquette isn't going to do you much good. On the other hand, if you're more interested in staying out of a knife fight, that book is very good.

First, here's the road map:

Alpha/beta behavior: *Cheap Shots, Ambushes, and Other Lessons: A Down and Dirty Book on Streetfighting and Survival.*

Angles: *Knives, Knife Fighting, and Related Hassles: How to Survive a Real Knife Fight • Street E & E: Evading, Escaping, and Other Ways to Save Your Ass When Things Get Ugly • Winning a Street Knife Fight: Realistic Offensive Techniques (video).*

Avoiding trouble: *Cheap Shots, Ambushes, and Other Lessons: A Down and Dirty Book on Streetfighting and Survival.*

Boomtown/borderlands: *Violence, Blunders, and Fractured Jaws: Advanced Awareness Techniques and Street Etiquette* • *Street E & E: Evading, Escaping, and Other Ways to Save Your Ass When Things Get Ugly.*

Checks/counters/blocks: *Cheap Shots, Ambushes, and Other Lessons: A Down and Dirty Book on Street-fighting and Survival* • *Knives, Knife Fighting, and Related Hassles: How to Survive a Real Knife Fight* • *Fists, Wits, and a Wicked Right: Surviving on the Wild Side of the Street* • *Winning a Street Knife Fight: Realistic Offensive Techniques (video).*

Knives: *Knives, Knife Fighting, and Related Hassles: How to Survive a Real Knife Fight* • *Winning a Street Knife Fight: Realistic Offensive Techniques (video).*

Maulers: *Cheap Shots, Ambushes, and Other Lessons: A Down and Dirty Book on Streetfighting and Survival* • *Fists, Wits, and a Wicked Right: Surviving on the Wild Side of the Street* • *Floor Fighting: Stompings, Maimings, and Other Things to Avoid When a Fight Goes to the Ground.*

Pivoting: *Fists, Wits, and a Wicked Right: Surviving on the Wild Side of the Street* • *Winning a Street Knife Fight: Realistic Offensive Techniques (video)* • *Floor Fighting: Stompings, Maimings, and Other Things to Avoid When a Fight Goes to the Ground.*

Quarters: *Pool Cues, Beer Bottles, and Baseball Bats: Animal's Guide to Improvised Weapons for Self-Defense and Survival* • *Winning a Street Knife Fight: Realistic Offensive Techniques (video)* • *Street E & E: Evading,*

Escaping, and Other Ways to Save Your Ass When Things Get Ugly.

Range: *Pool Cues, Beer Bottles, and Baseball Bats: Animal's Guide to Improvised Weapons for Self-Defense and Survival* • *Surviving a Street Knife Fight* • *Street E & E: Evading, Escaping, and Other Ways to Save Your Ass When Things Get Ugly.*

Recognizing trouble: *Cheap Shots, Ambushes, and Other Lessons: A Down and Dirty Book on Streetfighting and Survival* • *Violence, Blunders, and Fractured Jaws: Advanced Awareness Techniques and Street Etiquette* • *Street E & E: Evading, Escaping, and Other Ways to Save Your Ass When Things Get Ugly.*

Recovery: *Barroom Brawling: The Art of Staying Alive in Beer Joints, Biker Bars, and Other Fun Places (video)* • *Street E & E: Evading, Escaping, and Other Ways to Save Your Ass When Things Get Ugly.*

Slap Blocks: *Cheap Shots, Ambushes, and Other Lessons: A Down and Dirty Book on Streetfighting and Survival* • *Knives, Knife Fighting, and Related Hassles: How to Survive a Real Knife Fight* • *Winning a Street Knife Fight: Realistic Offensive Techniques (video)* • *Fists, Wits, and a Wicked Right: Surviving on the Wild Side of the Street.*

Targeting: *(bare-handed) Fists, Wits, and a Wicked Right: Surviving on the Wild Side of the Street* • *(with weapons) Pool Cues, Beer Bottles, and Baseball Bats: Animal's Guide to Improvised Weapons for Self-Defense and Survival* • *Fists, Wits, and a Wicked Right* • *Winning a Street Knife Fight: Realistic Offensive Techniques (video).*

Weapons (general): *Pool Cues, Beer Bottles, and*

Baseball Bats: Animal's Guide to Improvised Weapons for Self-Defense and Survival • *Winning a Street Knife Fight: Realistic Offensive Techniques (video)*.

Women and Violence: *Cheap Shots, Ambushes, and Other Lessons: A Down and Dirty Book on Streetfighting and Survival* • *Street E & E: Evading, Escaping, and Other Ways to Save Your Ass When Things Get Ugly.*

Below is a listing organized by the sort of situation you can find yourself in. I've listed the books and videos in the order of importance based on what I think will achieve the best results.

You just want to stay out of trouble:
1) *Cheap Shots, Ambushes, and Other Lessons: A Down and Dirty Book on Streetfighting and Survival,* 2) *Violence, Blunders, and Fractured Jaws: Advanced Awareness Techniques and Street Etiquette,* 3) *Street E & E: Evading, Escaping, and Other Ways to Save Your Ass When Things Get Ugly,* 4) *Winning a Street Knife Fight: Realistic Offensive Techniques (video).*

You want to stay out of trouble, but it's not too likely to happen:
1) *Cheap Shots, Ambushes, and Other Lessons: A Down and Dirty Book on Streetfighting and Survival,* 2) *Winning a Street Knife Fight: Realistic Offensive Techniques (video),* 3) *Street E & E: Evading, Escaping, and Other Ways to Save Your Ass When Things Get Ugly,* 4) *Floor Fighting: Stompings, Maimings, and Other Things to Avoid When a Fight Goes to the Ground,* 5) *Fists, Wits, and a Wicked Right: Surviving on the Wild Side of the Street.*

You wanted to stay out of trouble but didn't; now you need to survive:
1) *Street E & E: Evading, Escaping, and Other Ways to*

Save Your Ass When Things Get Ugly, 2) *Winning a Street Knife Fight: Realistic Offensive Techniques (video)*, 3) *Floor Fighting: Stompings, Maimings, and Other Things to Avoid When a Fight Goes to the Ground*, 4) *Cheap Shots, Ambushes, and Other Lessons: A Down and Dirty Book on Streetfighting and Survival*, 5) *Fists, Wits, and a Wicked Right: Surviving on the Wild Side of the Street*.

You're likely to end up in it, and you're not adverse to cracking a few heads:
1) *Cheap Shots, Ambushes, and Other Lessons: A Down and Dirty Book on Streetfighting and Survival*, 2) *Floor Fighting: Stompings, Maimings, and Other Things to Avoid When a Fight Goes to the Ground*, 3) *Fists, Wits, and a Wicked Right: Surviving on the Wild Side of the Street*, 4) *Street E & E: Evading, Escaping, and Other Ways to Save Your Ass When Things Get Ugly*, 5) *Violence, Blunders, and Fractured Jaws: Advanced Awareness Techniques and Street Etiquette*, 6) *Barroom Brawling: The Art of Staying Alive in Beer Joints, Biker Bars, and Other Fun Places (video)*.

You live in a place where fighting is a fun pastime:
1) *Cheap Shots, Ambushes, and Other Lessons: A Down and Dirty Book on Streetfighting and Survival*, 2) *Fists, Wits, and a Wicked Right: Surviving on the Wild Side of the Street*, 3) *Floor Fighting: Stompings, Maimings, and Other Things to Avoid When a Fight Goes to the Ground*, 4) *Violence, Blunders, and Fractured Jaws: Advanced Awareness Techniques and Street Etiquette*, 5) *Barroom Brawling: The Art of Staying Alive in Beer Joints, Biker Bars, and Other Fun Places (video)*.

You live in a place where fighting is not for fun but is deadly serious:
1) *Cheap Shots, Ambushes, and Other Lessons: A Down and Dirty Book on Streetfighting and Survival*, 2) *Winning*

a Street Knife Fight: Realistic Offensive Techniques (video),
3) *Street E & E: Evading, Escaping, and Other Ways to
Save Your Ass When Things Get Ugly*, 4) *Floor Fighting:
Stompings, Maimings, and Other Things to Avoid When a
Fight Goes to the Ground*, 5) *Pool Cues, Beer Bottles, and
Baseball Bats: Animal's Guide to Improvised Weapons for
Self-Defense and Survival* 6) *Fists, Wits, and a Wicked
Right: Surviving on the Wild Side of the Street.*

You're in an area where knives are common:
1) *Winning a Street Knife Fight: Realistic Offensive
Techniques (video)*, 2) *Street E & E: Evading, Escaping, and
Other Ways to Save Your Ass When Things Get Ugly.*

You want to carry a knife:
1) *Knives, Knife Fighting, and Related Hassles: How to
Survive a Real Knife Fight*, 2) *Winning a Street Knife
Fight: Realistic Offensive Techniques (video).*

You want to know weapons:
1) *Knives, Knife Fighting, and Related Hassles: How to
Survive a Real Knife Fight*, 2) *Winning a Street Knife Fight:
Realistic Offensive Techniques (video). 3) Pool Cues, Beer
Bottles, and Baseball Bats: Animal's Guide to Improvised
Weapons for Self-Defense and Survival* 4) *Fists, Wits, and a
Wicked Right: Surviving on the Wild Side of the Street.*

You're part of the reason your neighborhood is so
dangerous:
Read them all.

Introduction

1) OOPS!
2) Oh, shit!

—The two most common "last words" heard on black box recordings of crashed airplanes

I recently read a book in which the hero waxes poetic about how there is no moment of enlightenment more terrible than when you realize your parents are simple human beings. I disagree. I think the most terrible moment of enlightenment is when you realize you're outflanked, outfucked, and outgunned. While I could wax poetic about earth-shaking flashes of enlightenment regarding violence, the bottom line is, sooner or later, every man has the sickening realization that he brought a knife to a gun fight. If you don't have your ducks in line when this happens, it could be the last realization of your life. This book is

1

about what you can do to survive just such a moment. So without further ado, let's get quacking!

A book on street evasion and escape can neither be written nor understood by someone who has excessive sperm pressure on the brain. I personally have no problem admitting that I have been in situations that scared the shit out of me. After doing quick calculations on the probability of my survival if I stayed and did the Macho Shuffle, I have run like hell! Yes, folks, the big, bad Animal has run fiercely. Especially when I was outnumbered. The only times I faced down numerous opponents was when I couldn't find any other way around it. I was stuck, the shit was about to go down, and I had to stop it.

Having lived the kind of life I have, I gave up any delusions of immortality years ago. I freely admit I get my panties in a wad when I hear the bumblebee buzz of a bullet whiz by or when someone pulls a knife and wants to play show and tell with my vital organs. I got some news for you folks: that's a normal reaction, regardless of how much you've been through. For those of you who still feel bad because you can't knock bullets out of the air with your dick, don't worry—you are neither alone nor less of a man because you get scared when confronted with violence.

In fact, anyone who claims never to have been scared in a violent situation is one or more of the following: 1) a liar, 2) too stupid to realize what was happening, 3) a psychotic, or 4) a person who has never been in serious shit before. Number four is the guy who likes to fight and thinks it's a game right up until the moment he gets mauled by someone who doesn't. This is the guy who's always decided when it's time to scrap (usually when the odds are in his favor) and hasn't had the experience of someone competent getting the first shot off first. It's easy to handle an attack you see coming from a mile away; it's the shadow with a shotgun near your parking space that's hard to survive. Unfortunately, Number 4 is usually the guy who is going around calling other people sissies for being scared.

Until you've had someone seriously try to kill you, seen someone's guts fall out as a result of a knife slash, watched friends die, or gone into the hospital with a permanently mauled body, it's easy to think that fighting is nothing more than a Hollywood punch-out. Face it, in comparison to that, punching each other is a fucking game! I don't care how bad someone thinks he is because he's been in all these tournaments; until someone has gone through the shit, he ain't qualified to tell me what I should feel about it! And that goes double for Mr. Macho telling you what you should feel about it, Buckaroo!

The reality of it all is sooner or later everybody loses (or gets hurt in) a fight. It is the nature of the beast. No matter how good a fighter someone is, it'll happen. Real fighting is a game of Russian roulette, where sooner or later there's a bullet in the barrel for someone involved. Whether that someone survives this incident depends on two things: 1) who he's up against and 2) what he does when he realizes what's happening. These factors can have life or death consequences, or you can just get the shit beat out of you. On the other hand, if Allah has favored you with common sense, you might realize it's time to amscray before you get your dick chewed off.

Personally, I don't trust anyone who has never had the realization of his own mortality, either by losing a fight or getting into a situation over his head. Experiences like that are the seeds of common sense. Until someone has chewed dirt, he's going to think he's Superman, and in the real world, you don't want to be hanging with a wannabe man of steel. A guy with delusions of grandeur is not going to know when it's time to *vamoose*! This ignorance is not only going to get his ass in trouble, he's going to share the wealth with anyone with him. He may think he's bulletproof, but I'm standing next to him and I have no such delusions. Namely because I know what bad shots people are. I also know how often people back up on you when they lose the first round. This time, though, they're bringing artillery.

It's an old street maxim that the safest place to be during a gang shooting is the intended target. The reason for this is most gangsters are such bad shots that they'll miss the person they're aiming for. The bad news is anyone standing next to the guy they're shooting at is screwed. Anything beyond a range of 10 feet and it's a total wild card as to who's going to get hit. Now you can see why I'd have problems with someone like that. In his stupidity, the guy may set up someone else to get shot. When the fecal matter is heading toward the oscillating blades, that guy is *not* going to make the best long-term survival decisions. In fact, he's going to drag anyone with him into the storm.

The other extreme is the guy who bolts at the first sign of trouble, leaving his partners in the lurch. When I was a young fighting buck, I was in the habit of advertising my machismo by wearing a black kimono as street wear. (Can you say "suicidal," boys and girls? I was a 17-year-old dude, what can I say?) I was in a mall clothing store with a friend. This guy was okay, but he was not a fighter. We were standing at a clothes rack in the middle of the store. I was looking down at a shirt on the rack and asking him about it, when suddenly I heard a "BAM!" right in front of me. I looked up and saw four black dudes, one of who had slammed his leather-gloved hands down on top of the clothes rack.

"You in the arts, Cuz?" he drawled.

4

My immediate reaction was to say to myself, "Oh shit." These guys were part of the Crips local to the mall. These homies weren't from the west side or the shoreline contingents where I was known. Worse yet, they were hunting. My kimono had acted like a red cape held up to a bull. Well, if you aren't fishing for trouble, don't bait the hook. I had baited the hook, so I had to deal with it. It was time to stand up or stand aside.

Having determined that, I thought to myself, "Four against two isn't too bad." So my eyes narrowed, and I said, "Yeah."

It was at that moment that I realized something was seriously wrong. I can usually sense when someone is near me, and I was getting a blank spot from my nines. I checked to my left, where my friend had been a mere moment ago, and I saw he was gone. I looked farther and saw the son of a bitch had rabbited on me all the way across the store. He was looking through another rack and watching me out of the corner of his eye. When I looked at him, he guiltily dropped his eyes to the floor. At that moment I knew that I was alone on this one. It had suddenly become four against one.

"What style?" the leader asked.

Suddenly, my answer of "shotokan" seemed real weak, and I began to cast for a way to exit quickly. "What style you in?" I responded. He answered me, and I began to talk my way out of it with comments like, "Good style!" and "Who you study under?"

To make a long story short, I ended up verbally tap dancing out of the situation. I admit, I did handle it, just not the way that my machismo wanted me to. I was left in the lurch because my friend had beaten me off the starting line and left me alone. The guy bugged out on me in the one way I'm going to tell you not to do to your worst enemy. *You never leave a partner flapping in the breeze!* If you're going to run, you always take your partner! Even if you gotta drag the son of a bitch by his collar. Bugging out is fine, but you don't leave your own! If the person standing next to you isn't one of your own, at least tell him/her before you leave.[1]

The important lesson of this book is that there are different ways of bugging out of a situation. Nobody calls a mongoose a coward when he dodges a cobra strike, yet many people think that doing a strategic withdrawal in a conflict situation is a sign of cowardice. In my book, if you've realized that you're outgunned in a situation, heading for the hills is a surefire sign of intelligence! If you've walked into a situation where there's no way you're going to win, fall back and regroup.

Inherent in human beings is a thing called the fight-or-flight syndrome. It is as basic as our sex drive and other instincts. In fact, it is how our sense of self-preservation manifests itself on a basic level. This instinct means that when faced with danger we either beat feet or attack. There are certain physiological responses that go with it, including the root of the terms "scared the shit out of someone" or "madder than shit," both of which involve voiding excess weight.[2] Most people, when they think of this fight/flight reaction, consider it an either/or proposition; either you're going for blood, or you're hauling ass out of there.

What a thunderin' herd of people don't understand is that you can mix and match these two things. You can run with the ferocity of a wolf and, when the situation changes in your favor, turn on those who are chasing you. *Anyone who chases you does so at his own peril!*

The Mongols were particularly adept at nailing someone who was dumb enough to chase them. A common trick was to ride away until their pursuit got strung out behind them. Then the Genghis boys would suddenly turn and, WHAMO! My personal favorite was when a pack of European knights chased after them. The Mongols and their lighter ponies shot through a bog that mired down the knights and their big war-horses. Once the flowers of chivalry were stuck like flies on flypaper, the horde turned and started doing target practice. This sort of fighting is what was responsible for their conquering more land than anyone else in history. This is also the essence of street escape and evasion. You're not fleeing; you're staying alive long enough to be able to turn the tables.

One of the things that makes me different than most self-defense teachers is I know it's a different type of fighting out in the street. Tradition and style are fine, but if you want to stay alive, you'd better train what you're going to meet up with. When I was a young pup hopping in the streets of Venice, California, we started using weapons. That seriously affected the way I look at conflict. I don't care how tough you are, a knife in the guts will mess up your day. In light of this, I fight like the mongoose against the cobra. Unlike a king snake, which is immune to the rattlesnake's venom, the mongoose could be killed by the cobra's bite. One hit and it's all over for Mr. Mongy. Therefore, when the cobra strikes, the mongoose dodges. Then, once it is off the line of danger, the mongoose strikes and kills the snake. That's how something that isn't immune to snake venom can survive hunting snakes, and that's how you can survive a street situation.

As much as it may piss off karate buffs and he-men who want to play bare-handed macho games, there is a bottom-line reality that is occurring in America: *criminals use weapons!* God created all men equal, but Colonel Colt guaranteed it. A street dude with a weapon, a little experience, and the willingness to use it is more than a match for a black belt. So much for the Bruce Lee fantasy. Also (surprise, surprise), different ethnic groups (a member of which may or may not be involved in "criminal" activity) automatically use weapons in conflicts. Even the most mellow grandfather of the group will snatch up a weapon as a first move. I'm talking there might as well be an equal sign inserted there: "group = weapons."

What all of this means is, regardless of what you think is going on, you can suddenly find yourself in way over your head. This is the terrible moment of realization that I mentioned earlier. In situations like this, you have to do something other than what got you into the mess in the first place. I don't care what anybody else says, *if you find yourself facing a weapon bare-handed, get out of there as fast as you can!*

When it comes to weapons, unless you want a parade of slow marchin' and loud singing, you have to adopt a new attitude. That's the mongoose 'tude. When you back up on them, they are going to regret starting this dance. But, in the meantime, if you ain't there, they can't hurt you!

This also applies when four or five people decide that tonight's entertainment is stomping you into a pancake. In situations like this, putting your chin out and bravely stepping forth is tantamount to suicide. Just like a guerrilla fighter has stacked the deck in his favor before he moves, the street dude has done the same. Believe me when I say that if the deck weren't stacked in both of these situations, they wouldn't have moved in the first place. Knowing you've been set up to begin with should remove any hesitation you might have about getting out of there.

The problem comes in when the only thing being taught as self-defense is exactly what will get you killed. Face it, karate is head-to-head fighting (or, as a friend of mine says, "karate is punishment"). An important safety tip is that people teach what they're good at, not what you need to know. While stud muffins may want to teach you to do a toe-to-toe, the bad guy is going to be launching a guerrilla action. Karate doesn't teach you how to strike from behind, strike unexpectedly, fight dirty, and maul your opponent. Streetfighting does. Why study for something that the other guy isn't going play along with? You're trained for a stand-up fight, and he's trained for treachery. Guess who's going to lose?

Let's look at the sterling example of this scenario, Vietnam. American military, a definite kick-anybody's-ass-in-a-straight-up-rumble sort of group, met up with a group that said, "You're nuts if you think we're going to fight on your terms!" Little brown brother chose when and where he was going to hit. When he did hit, he had every card stacked in his favor. When it turned against him, he slipped out the back door! It was hit and run, hide and seek all the way! When they weren't attacking, they were doing innocent Little Bo Peep imitations among the civilians.[3] Every time the North Vietnamese Army (NVA) tried a stand-up fight with the American forces, it got torn into confetti. Yet, the ongoing guerrilla warfare was tearing the shit out of the American ground troops at every turn.

But wait a minute—which people were the most effective against the Vietcong? The ones who adopted the same tactics. Hit and run, hide and seek! The U.S. Special Forces were feared by both the North Vietnamese and the Vietcong because our guys fought just as nasty and smart as they did. By the time people woke up to the fact that they were being attacked, it was over, and the other team was gone. If the SEALs, Green Berets, Rangers, and LRRPs can fight and run, run and fight, so can you!

It isn't a ground acquisition game in the street, it's guerrilla warfare! Hit and run. In order to make it out there, you have to quit thinking like a grunt and start thinking like a member of your favorite elite force. It's a game of predator/prey, with who's who switching off often and unexpectedly. One of the reasons Special Forces are so good at what they do is they can turn from hunted to hunter at a split second. You chase one of those teams at your own peril.

Now that I have expressed the basic mental attitude that a person must have in order to be good at street escape and evasion, let's look at more pedestrian matters. This book is broken down into four basic sections. The first is based on *personal evasion*. That's when you're suddenly facing the problem up close. Either the guy's suddenly gone for a weapon or you've turned the corner and stepped into it. The second is *hot pursuit*. This is when you've survived initial contact and you're hotfooting it with them after you. The third is *fox and hound*, a standing situation where you have someone gunning for you (including minions of the law). This is when you are doing the dance of death with an identified enemy for a set period of time. The fourth is *Boomtown*. This consists of tips for those of you who are living the wild life and want to keep it up for a while. This is more a long-term survival issue.

Now, once again, I have to say the immortal words. You can recite them along with me if you want: 1) There ain't no guarantees in a fight; 2) I don't know everything there is about fighting—nobody does; 3) It's awareness that will keep you alive out there; and 4) If something in this book doesn't work for you, toss it out. Remember, it's your ass, Cochise, you say when.

Notes

1. Like the groundskeeper did for me and my crew at the Crip funeral. See *Violence, Blunders, and Fractured Jaws.*

2. In fact you can tell if the guy's really been through the mill by watching his reaction to the term, "I ain't got a hard-on with you." If he thinks that's funny, he hasn't been there. If he's been there, he knows what the term means and will often reconsider tying up with you, as an erection is another physiological reaction to combat.

3. So-called fair play says you can't shoot someone who isn't threatening you at the exact moment, at least according to laws of "police action warfare" and of the United States. The sucker may be guilty as hell, but you can't touch him after the fact. This is why the SODDI ("Some Other Dude Did It") defense is used so much. Unless he's got a weapon in hand, he's innocent.

Those Oh-So-Intimate Moments

I was sitting there chewing the fat with someone who's been through hell. The guy is former military internal affairs and ex-DEA. He's played tag with the real bad boys. He's got the marks to prove it, too. For years, we'd run in the same circles, yet we'd never sat down and pow-wowed, even though we both had major reputations. This was the first time he and I had ever gotten to know each other personally. Naturally, there was the sniffing-out period, during which he looked at me and said, "I don't see any knife scars."

I looked at him and said, "That's because I knew to back up!" I then went on to explain to him that if someone got the drop on me and I didn't have anyone to protect, I got the fuck out of there ASAP. I had nothing to prove by staying there and hashing it out with an ambusher.

He got this wistful expression on his face for a second and said in a quiet voice, "I could never do that. . . ." (It was like backpedaling was an entirely new concept to him. In truth, it was. Unlike me, even when the shit went down against him he still had to advance. Then his eyes snapped up, and I was looking into the eyes of a guy who had mauled more than a few people.) "I had to stick around," he said.

"Man that was your job," I responded. "You had to stay. My only job was saving my ass!"

To this day, every time I see this guy, he shakes his head and says in amazement, "I could never run away." Thus far I've refrained from pointing out to him that not only have I been shot and stabbed fewer times, I also wasn't the one who had to stand around holding my intestines in while waiting for the ambulance. This sort of proves there is something to be said for my system.

The problem that most people have is they lack an operating system for extreme situations. They have never taken their thinking process past a certain point. It only goes so far, then they categorize everything beyond that as a hazy "over there." Over there doesn't have any definitions, just general assumptions, which are often wildly wrong.[1] If you're going to make it out in the Boomtown, you need to keep going past normal. Some people can't even imagine running away, period. Other people just leave it at "I'll just run." That seems sufficient until the person actually attempts it. The process of "just running" turns out to be more complicated than they thought. There are techniques and stages in the process. Squirrely as it may sound, what most people consider to be the entire process, I consider only the middle stages. If you want to make it out there, you have to look at both the beginning and the end.

Most people when they think about "just running" think only of escape (i.e., the hazy idea of "If something goes wrong, I'll just run like hell!"). That's as far as they take it. Well I got some news for you people— there's a good chance that ain't going to cut it. The term evade and escape is a two-point system. In the military it means evade contact and then escape. When those two points are mixed, it makes the whole shebang a lot easier. Also in the military sense, it means buying yourself time and distance by making your opponents reluctant to chase you at full speed.

While it also means the same thing in the street, there's a little bit more. First off, you must avoid damage; then you can escape. If you're gushing blood, you're not going to be in the best of shape to make an effective getaway. Not only are you going into shock, both from trauma and loss of blood, but you aren't going to be thinking straight. Even the dumbest street hood can usually outthink someone in shock. If you're wounded, the only thing between you and the great hereafter is what is going on in the other guy's mind. If he decides to split, you're safe. If he decides to continue the issue, y'all are screwed.

When it comes to evasion and escape, most people think that running away is ground zero. *NOT!* However, since this is what is commonly thought to be the case, we're going to have to start somewhere nearby, or it'll seem like I'm off in La-La Land. The stuff we're going to be covering in these first few chapters is actually in the middle of the whole process. We're going to start at initial contact and work from there. However, to someone who is good at street E & E, the sequence reads like this: 1) Boomtown, 2) initial contact, 3) hot pursuit, 4) fox and hound. By the end of this book you'll see why that makes sense. Like all of my books, this one should be read two or three times to get exactly what it is that I'm getting at.

We've already decided it's easier to escape from a situation if you're not hurt. Therefore let's look at the basis of this whole situation. When most people are asked what they would do if attacked by a knife or club, they usually respond by saying, "I'd defend myself." Now, I have to ask you, what the hell does that mean? Does it mean kung-fuing your attacker? Does it mean running like hell? What? Think about that in your own head for awhile before you read on.

I can tell you what it means in my system of "Applied Self-Defense." Before you consider doing anything else, your first priority is *neutralize the threat!* You do what you need to do to keep from getting hurt by that particular attack. This does not mean you immediately start pounding on someone until he's flat. Nor does it mean you immediately run like hell. It means, before you even consider doing anything else, you make sure your ass is safe from the specific attack!

It is incredible how important this issue is—and how often it's underemphasized. I want to point out the different results this emphasis can have. The guy I mentioned previously had training from both the military and the DEA. The idea behind both was to take the target down. Priority number one was the take-down of an assigned enemy, not the personal safety of the operative. On the other hand, most of my serious conflicts were geared to surviving to my next blowjob (getting, not giving). The result of this attitude has been that all of my serious trips to the hospital have involved taking someone else. Usually the wounded someone was trained in the other system.[2]

When it comes to the shit storm, the aforementioned guy and I had totally different priorities. This doesn't reflect on his native intelligence or my respect for him, but it does show that he was trained to be safe by flattening a threat rather than neutralizing it. The problem with that system is that while you're taking the person down, all too often he's getting a piece of you, too. Unless the guy has been brainwashed by TV, it's going to take between 10 and 120 seconds for even a bullet to incapacitate him, even if he's fatally shot. A person can do a lot of damage to you in that time. (See *Handgun Stopping Power*, by Evan Marshall and Edwin Sanow, published by Paladin Press.) That's why cops don't get closer than 21 feet to a guy with a knife. Even with a few slugs in him, a guy with a knife can take a shooter with him. Taking someone out is a whole lot slower than you think, and if you haven't neutralized his counterattack, you're in some deep kimchi.[3]

On the other hand, once a threat is neutralized, *then* you have the choice of staying around to hammer or getting the hell out of there. In either case, neutralizing the threat is only a short-term solution for the immediate problem. It hasn't stopped the scenario of being attacked, all it's done is stopped the specific move. It has bought you a moment to decide on what is the best course. If you choose to hang around, you're still running the risk of getting seriously hurt. Important safety tip here: *no matter how good you are, the odds are your "hammer" is not going to incapacitate the guy immediately.* In case you haven't noticed, being in close proximity to someone with a weapon who is pissed and hurt—but not incapacitated—is a good way to get yourself torn up. There's an old saying, "Accept you will be cut in a knife fight." This is true, but I put a qualifier on that statement: "If you stay around to fight . . ." Bottom line here, folks: it's when you hang around that you can get hurt! If there is anything that pisses me off about the bullshit that most martial art schools peddle as self-defense, this is it: either they ignore weapons entirely or they teach people to charge in against one blindly! Do what you have to do to break contact and continue mission! There is a time to counterattack, and there is a time to retreat! Not knowing which is which will get you killed.

The DEA guy is right—he never had a choice. He had to charge in, regardless of what was going on. However, I—and I assume you—*do* have a choice. Knowing that, the question now becomes how you avoid getting mauled out there.

I used to travel around with a pack of drunken psychotics I called my friends. Our idea of fun was to get rip-roaring drunk, crawl into rusty armor, and hack away at each other with real swords. Now I had some fencing training, but it wasn't until I had someone try to split my skull with a broadsword that I realized something really important.[4] While there are literally thousands of ways to attack someone, they can all be broken down into astoundingly basic categories. A swinging attack is coming in from the same angle if it's a knife, fist, club, or bullwhip. How the person moves around the attack is going to vary radically, but the basic line that attack is coming in on is going to stay the same.

Well I thought this was a really great bit of news because it simplified my life incredibly. I used the clock system to describe an attack coming at me (e.g., at noon or three o'clock). I knew which blocks worked in which time zones. I did get to the point eventually where I'd drink a beer while holding off a sword attack (was I cocky, or what?). Then one day I met a practitioner of kali, and he told me I was talking about the nine angles. Wow! Nearly 20 years of work and I find out that someone has already invented the damn thing! Actually, my little tail wagged in joy when I heard this bit of news, and I made a beeline out to find out what the other guys knew about it.

Well surprise, surprise—those rascally Filipinos had caught onto something a few hundred years before the rest of the world and had then gone on to do the unthinkable. They put it in a simple, easily understood format. Despite the brouhaha about karate and taekwon do, the Filipinos had devised a nastier and more effective fighting form around a concept so easy and basic that a rock could understand it. They broke it down to nine angles you can be attacked from.[5] I defy anyone to find a physical attack, either bare-handed or with a weapon, that isn't covered by this simple system.

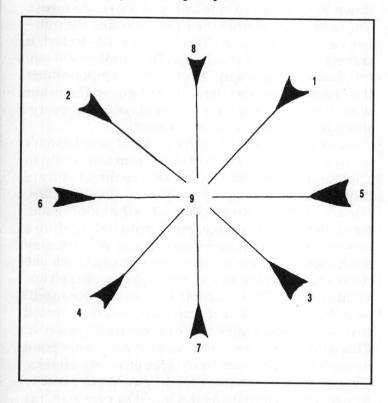

Nine angles.

That's it, folks—every way, shape, or form you're going to be attacked by is in these nine basic angles. The only thing that can change on you is the level. A number 1 angle is the same if it is going toward your head or your knee! A bullet (unless it's a ricochet) is going to come at you on number 9. If you want to get extreme, a bomb dropped from a plane is coming at you on number 8. Nifty idea, isn't it? It's so much easier than learning how to defend against 52,000 different attacks!

When you break it down into the basics, it's an "x," "+," and poke. I'm talking diagonals (an up-down line), a side-to-side line, and a straight thrust. That's it! Starting from the right shoulder, the number 1 angle is a diagonal downward slash. In fact, it travels along the same line as the number 4 slash, but down instead of up. Everything except number 9 is the same as another one, but going the other way. This incredibly simple formula contains everything you're going to meet out there!

Now the really exciting news. Most people aren't good enough to suddenly shift from one angle to another in midflight. That means the threat you are facing is usually going to be only on one line! One line, one attack! God, I love it! This takes the whole giant, terrifying furball of a fight and breaks it down into a sequential chain of individual events! While it may seem blindingly fast, most people actually attack one move at a time. One attack, one angle; another attack, another angle. It's incredible how many people will attack on the same line repeatedly. Often the guy will throw the same punch two or three times in a row. That's definitely the same line. Few people are good enough to chain more than three effective attacks. Usually after two shots or so, the guy has to pause to figure out what to do next. Or just as common, his third or fourth blow will be weak because he's lost control of his physics. When it comes to running into someone who can attack on two angles at once effectively, we're talking hen's teeth. The feint, or set-up punch, isn't the real attack; it's what's coming next that is the real threat. Even then, 999 out of a thousand times, feints/setups don't come at the same time as the real attack. When people talk about being attacked, they are confusing the whole scenario with the component parts.

What I am telling you here is, while it looks confusing as hell at first, it's simpler than most people think. That's because you're actually dealing with a chain of events that can be broken down into individual links. What you have to worry about in a sequential series of events is one move at a time! Taking things in smaller steps is easier to handle than a giant ball of chaotic possibilities.

One thing my lady Tracy loves about me is that I'm not a football fan. In fact, to show you how big of a nonfan I am, I was recently shocked to discover that the NFL and AFL merged.[6] On the other hand, I do love a good fight. There is nothing like a good old-fashioned knock-down-drag-out brawl to get my blood pumping. I don't like karate tournaments to fulfill this fetish of mine. Boxing is good, and I watch it when I can, but I prefer actually going to the events. What really did it for me was muay thai bouts. L.A. has a large Thai population, and those little suckers go for blood. (I used to take Tracy until a riot broke out at one and she refused to attend anymore. Women are so fussy.)

The reason I bring up professional sports is to turn your attention to them. They are a great way to learn that attacks are sequential chains rather than simply giant hairballs of danger. Plonk yourself down in front of the TV and watch some fighting (beer, munchies, and some buddies make it even more fun). Look for the sequential character of the fight and guess which angles are being used. Not only will this prove that there are seldom simultaneous attacks and that attacks do come in on certain angles, but you can learn all of this without getting your head bashed in. It's the guys in the ring that are getting bashed while you're learning this stuff. By observing this, you train your mind to watch for these sorts of developments.[7]

Dear old Peyton Quinn once said the most common street attacks are a straight punch and a hook. He's right—give that man a cigar. Those are the two most common bare-handed attacks. It breaks down into a number 9 (straight shot to the face) and number 5 (hook to the head). With a club, the most common attacks are number 1 (diagonal downward strike) and number 5 (baseball bat swing). A number 7 (direct overhand downward strike) comes in a close third in the club category. With a knife, the most common attacks are number 9 (stab) and number 5 (horizontal slash), although a wobbly number 3 (upward diagonal slash from the right hip) is also common. Usually, however, it is more of a low-line number 5. As I've mentioned before, a bullet comes in on angle number 9.[8]

Now let's take a look at those different attacks and see why they would be the same angles. Basically, anything that comes in on a horizontal plane from the guy's right is a number 5. Punch, knife slash, or club, they all follow the same line. Where people get confused with all of this is the guy has to hold his body, arm, and wrist differently, depending on what he is using. A knifer will have to hold his arm bent with his palm up to slash. Meanwhile, a puncher will be holding his palm down, and his elbow will be on the same line as his fist and shoulder when he strikes. A guy with a club will either be holding his hand in a modified knife strike, or he will be using a two-handed baseball swing when he moves.

Guess what, people? Once again, it's time for the "Animal-says-I-need-to-practice-this" routine. Even if you don't practice any of the other physical techniques that I've ever talked about, I highly recommend you familiarize yourself with these angles. Kali has predetermined ways to dodge them, which, for the most part, I agree with. Learning these angles is step one of a two-part process. This is important in that you need to know instinctively which angle you're being threatened from. Before you can do that, though, you have to be able to recognize what's coming at you. Now you can do this one of two ways: 1) do what I did and go out and get the snot beat out of you until you subconsciously recognize the threat, or 2) practice the angles until you learn them. Show you're smarter than I was and do it the intelligent way.

This means you get to stand there counting off the angles and moving your hands along them (if you use a stick or knife it seems to work better). Count off the angles as you go, until you can do them without getting confused. At first you're going to have to practice these angles by yourself. If you've done too many drugs and your memory is shot, draw the pattern on the wall and follow it. If you can remember, do them in the air before you. Try to follow the lines as closely and tightly as you can. This is step one.

It's step two that really gets most people tripping over themselves. Where this system gets confusing is when you're facing another guy. Your number 1 is going to be moving from your right shoulder but landing on his left shoulder and vice versa. The actual dynamics are that the image is truly reversed on you. His number 1 is coming along your number 2 line, but it's a number 1 attack. How you handle a number 1 and a number 2 are completely different.

You see his number 1 as the same line as your number 2. This gets a thundering herd of people confused until you solve the problem with a friend. See, if you know how to dodge a number 1 angle, but your brain goes, "2—no, 1!" by the time you figure it out, you've been clobbered.

In the movie *Exposure* (the only good movie about knife fighting in my opinion), the heavy has the student practice in front of a mirror. I don't agree with that. The idea, as near as I can figure it out, is to teach the guy what the angles look like coming at you from the other side. This is better accomplished by doing it with a partner facing you as opposed to a mirror. This is all a roundabout way of saying get a friend and face each other, and both of you do it while counting out the sequence. The reason is, while mirrors reverse things, it's only a partial

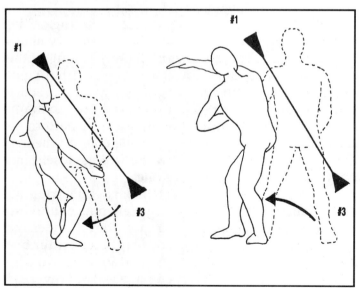

Dodging a number 1 or number 3 attack. Left: better position for counterstriking.
Right: better position for running.

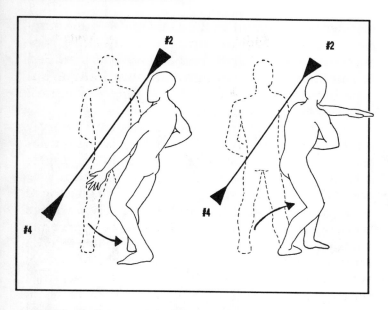

Dodging a number 2 or number 4 attack. Left: better position for counterstriking.
Right: better position for running.

reverse. When you are doing a number 1 angle, your mirror reflection is doing a whacked-out number 1 on you—not what number 1 *really* looks like coming at you. This is why you need another body. You need to see what it looks like coming at you and going away when you are saying number 1. Both of you are saying number 1 to get what it looks like on both ends firmly implanted in your noggins. Seeing a squirreled-out version in your mirror is going to confuse ya when you get into the real thing.

Now, the accepted ways to dodge attacks are pretty basic, and while I'm going to rattle them off here, I highly recommend you cruise out to the source of this system: kali/escrima/arnis and (I know, it isn't technically correct to include this with the Filipino styles) pentjak-silat.

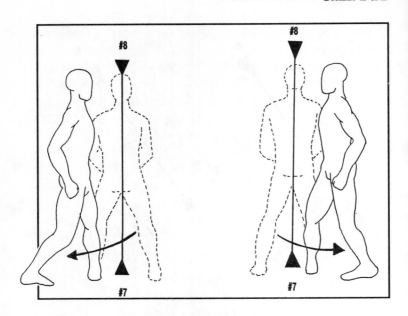

Dodging a number 7 or number 8 attack. (Also works on most number 9 attacks.)
Left: better position for counterstriking. Right: better position for running.

Now there are some variations I personally recommend, as they are subtle but important issues that are designed to aid and abet your bug-out. They have to do with angles number 1 and number 2. While the kali fighters usually stick around to finish the match, you have to understand that in a place where everyone carries a knife, knife fights are common. I don't know what it is, but there's just something about someone trying to stab you when you have a knife, too, that makes you want to stay around and show him the error of his ways. On the other hand, if he's the only one with the weapon, it's time to leave. As you can see, these variations make departure just a split second faster.

Another thing I have nattered on about is something called stance integrity. There is no easier way to

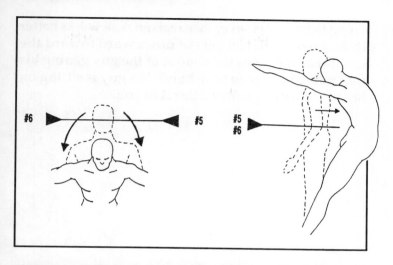

Dodging a number 5 or number 6 attack. Left: dangerous against a skilled fighter; only works against high 5 and 6 (but sometimes you gotta do what you gotta do). Right: safer.

set someone on his ass than by using his own body's construction against him. If you're fighting someone with three legs, you have either taken some seriously bad acid, or you turned left in the middle of a quantum worm hole. Generally, however, you can rely on your opponents having the prescribed number of feet and legs. Little bit of Pythagorean geometry here: if you have three points that are not in a line, you have a triangle.[9] If you have two separate points, you can draw a line between them. Point A and B, you got a line. Left and right foot, same thing—a line. This line creates a thing called stance integrity. Any force coming along this line can be resisted by the stability of the two points.

Any force coming in perpendicular (90 degrees) off this line is going to meet zippo resistance though. There's no stability from that angle. Putting it bluntly, unless the guy has got fast feet, the odds are that he's going to be on his ass or face real quick. It works better if the push/pull is directed downward toward the ground as it lessens the chance of the guy getting his foot moved faster to save him.[10] If a guy is sitting on his ass, he's not much of a threat to you.

Notes

1. Think about it for a second, what is life like in Indochina? Africa? India? Most people have a vague image of happy little natives running around in ethnic dress and then are shocked when they see pictures of modern buildings and Western clothing. Stanley Kubrick's *Full Metal Jacket* was filmed in an abandoned industrial area in England. Why? Because the movie was about an area of Vietnam which looked like that. That's the most obvious example of "over there hazy definitions." If you really want to mess with your head, what about concepts you hold?

2. All too often, the other guy has been torn up pretty bad. While it may look like I'm making light of it, taking friends to the hospital is not fun, folks.

3. Kimchi is fermented cabbage that has been pickled in garlic and hot peppers and buried for three months like sauerkraut. It smells like old gym socks fermented in garlic and Tabasco. It is the favored dish of psychos, Koreans, guys who have served overseas, and Klingons. Tracy will not allow me to eat it in the house or to kiss her for several hours after eating it. It is most definitely an acquired taste. Personally, I love the stuff with beer. One of my fondest memories is sitting around with the mad dog brigade with a full keg and a case of kimchi. The fact that we were eating it off our knives and had abandoned cups to merely pouring the beer down our throuts from the tap sort of added panache to the whole affair.

4. Aside from how quickly you can sober up when someone is swinging a three-pound piece of steel at your unprotected skull.

5. Although now there's debate between systems as to how many angles there actually are—up to 13 in some schools. I say shine it, the variations are just that.

6. Tim looked at me in disgust and said, "They

merged in the late '60s, Animal." How was I supposed to know? Last time I watched football the Minnesota Vikings were doing well.

7. It can also train you to look for holes in the guy's defenses. Try to guess where he is going to hit next. Good way to train without bleeding.

8. Except Chris Pfouts. He got shot in the leg on a number 7 (a downward-directed attack). Hear that, Chris, and you thought it was a .38. *Ha!*

9. There's a secret of fighting footwork in that statement for those of you of inquiring minds. Anytime you move just one foot, you are creating a triangle. You always want to leave a point of the triangle toward your opponent, not a face.

10. I've covered this topic more extensively in the video *Surviving a Street Knife Fight*. The information in the video *Barroom Brawling: The Art of Staying Alive in Beer Joints, Biker Bars, and Other Fun Places* makes a whole lot more sense if you integrate stance integrity into it.

CHAPTER TWO

Up Close and Personal

Once you have the basic angles down, you've really gotten most of the work done. After that everything is pretty much fine-tuning. Granted, it is fine-tuning that can get you killed, but it is still fine-tuning. I've talked myself blue in the face about pivoting in other books and videos, so I won't rehash it here, except to say that it is critical for you to have it down pat. In fact, this chapter is basically a rehash of many things that I've said elsewhere. This is the first time that I've brought them all together in one area, so it won't hurt to review them. And if you've missed the original book or video, this will catch you up and tell you what

31

you need to look into to find a fuller explanation of this information.[1] Then again, for you old-timers, I might just slip in a new concept just to mess with ya, so don't touch that dial!

Without belaboring the obvious, the best way not to get stomped is not to let someone get closer to you

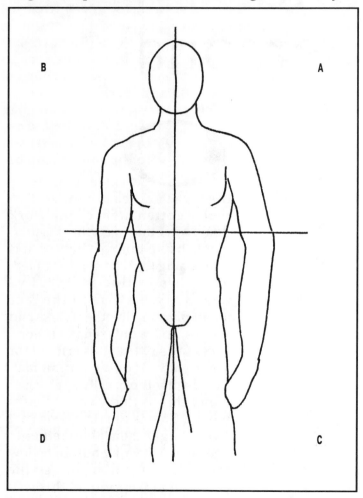

Quarters with letters.

than 5 feet. If someone insists on closing that distance, you know something is wrong, and you should adjust your thinking accordingly. A stranger approaching you on the street has no reason to come any closer than that. Another fun thing you should watch for is a group that tries to surround you while someone else is talking to you. The talker is distracting you while his homies get into position. Hands held out of sight, in pockets, and in weird ways are also signs of serious trouble looming on the horizon. If someone persists with any of these behaviors, you may want to bug out before he can actually initiate an attack.

Another thing that is rather useful is the four quarters that I mentioned in *Pool Cues, Beer Bottles, and Baseball Bats*.[2] Take your body and draw an imaginary line down the center. Now do the same thing but across your horizontal center.

You now have a basic schematic of your body. Simply put, if a quarter is being threatened, get it out of the way in the shortest way possible! With this model, many of the reasons for the kali defensive moves become clear. I've created a little model that will keep you from getting your head knocked in while you're figuring it out. Take a solid rectangular object that will stand up by itself, like a hardback book. Stand it up on the table in front of you and either actually draw or imagine the four quarters on it. A finger on your right hand becomes a club, while your left hand moves the object. Come at the object in the nine angles with your finger. Do it both high and low (like I said, a number 1 angle is a number 1 angle, whether it's coming at your head or your knee). When your right hand comes down to contact, have your left move the object out of the way along the shortest/safest route.

Remember, people aren't likely to change angles in mid-attack, but they are likely to keep on going along the same line! That means you can get one quarter out of the way and still leave another in danger along the same line of attack, only lower. Take the rectangle and come down at it on a #1 angle, thereby threatening the B section. Instead of pivoting to the right (the kali defense), try scooting the object to your left. As you'll see, B section is moved out of the way, but the D sector is still in danger if there's a follow-through on the attack (and if the object is a club or a bat, you can bet there will be). Now, if anyone walks in on you while you're doing this experiment, simply tell them you used to do a lot of drugs and you're having a flashback. It's easier than explaining why you're sitting there playing with your finger and a book. When you're done playing with the book, take those concepts you've learned and apply them to your own body.

The next key factor to all of this is using checks. Yes, boys and girls, you do get to use your hands during this process. It is, however, critical that you learn to use your body first. Don't rely only on your hands. I don't care what they say in the dojo, I've been out there in the Boomtown. *If you rely on your hands only, you're going to be dog meat real quick!* My video *Surviving a Street Knife Fight* offers the best description of these.

Something I disagree with in most martial arts schools is that they teach defense from the outside in. Generally, they start off with the aggressive nonsense first. Come on, folks, hitting someone is not defense, it's offense. By definition, defending yourself is preventing yourself from getting hurt, not hammering someone into the ground. The other "oops," as far I'm concerned, is that they first focus on moving the hands and arms. After a couple of months (sometimes years), they include defensive moves for the body. All in all, I consider this to be something like an egg—hard on the outside, but all it takes is a little pressure and everything is going to get gooey right quick.

What has made me extremely unpopular with the martial arts world is that one little question I so love to ask: "How about when he gets the drop on you?" You will notice I didn't say "if," I said "when." This is reality, folks, not the movies. In reality, if you can think it up, so can the other side.[3] The other guy isn't on your side like in a dojo, and he's going to be doing everything in his power to make you lose. With him working against you, the odds of him successfully messing your move up are seriously high.

As a matter of fact, I was talking to the weapons advisor on one of those big-name-movie-martial-artist flicks. He told me that the Mr. Macho Martial Artist was telling him how he could take his gun away. The guy said, "No you couldn't; I'd shoot you before you got close enough." Tall, dark, and arrogant Mr. MMA said, "I'd use my wasabe and move to the side." Whereupon the gun guy said, "And I'd use mine, move to the side, and still shoot you." While I won't name names, I have little to no use for the movie martial artists I have met. These suckers exemplify this sort of attitude. Unfortunately, they have bigger advertising budgets than I do, so the public thinks those movies are real.

Anyway, back to checks, blocks, and counters. Yes, you can use them, and against a weapon you had damn well better. Before you get to this point, though, I recommend you practice dodging with the angles and quarters. In fact, for training in both areas, I highly recommend you regress to the age of 7 to practice. I am talking about a pillow fight. If you feel that you are too old to be standing on your bed with a friend wailing around, then go out and buy some bitakkas (those foam rubber swords) and start practicing. When you get to the point where you can dodge most blows, then start adding in checks. (After all the time I used up explaining checks and slap blocks in other books and videos, I don't want anyone to write me and ask me to explain! Grrr!).

Now it's time to move onto another aspect, and that is recovery time. Recovery time is how long it takes someone to slow down an attack and change it into the next one. What the weapon is and how fast he can recover will affect how fast the next attack will occur. As I've said before, it's not likely that the guy is going to be able to shift in midswing. With training, or a light weapon, it is possible, but it's highly unlikely with an untrained individual. Even with small blades and razors, untrained people usually try to muscle through rather than slice. That means a longer recovery time than a trained person will need.[4]

Recovery time is usually shorter with smaller, lighter weapons. A guy can turn a number 5 back onto itself into a number 6 quicker with a knife than he can with a pool cue. This will determine how much time you have to decide what to do. My general rule of thumb is the shorter the recovery time, the better it is to get out of range fast. If you're up close with a guy with a knife, he's going to come back at you much faster than a guy with a pool cue. If you're thinking of hanging around and kung-fueying the guy, take that into consideration. To be safe, you have to drop a guy with a knife faster than you do the guy with the club.

Now let's look at something else that I brought up in *Pool Cues, Beer Bottles, and Baseball Bats*. The range of a weapon. What is the effective range of a knife? Usually arm's length plus a few inches.[5] That means anything in that range from far away to wrestling is a danger zone for a knife. That means to be out of the danger zone for a knife you have to be outside that range. Once more, if all else fails, quickly skipping back out of range is really effective. It's not real graceful, but oh, does it work well.

Now what about a pool cue? Unless you can really skip hard, you may actually help the guy crack your head open. Your real danger zone is about a foot to a foot and a half in from the tip. The same system of physics that applies to a record—oh, excuse me, I forgot this isn't the '70s anymore, a CD—applies to a swinging club. That is, while the rotation is the same, a point near the center is traveling slower than the outside edge of the CD. In order for the outside to travel the same distance, it must be traveling at a higher speed. Therefore, unlike a knife, with a club there are two safety zones: 1) outside the range of the weapon (arm + whatever length of club), and 2) inside the arc at a point of slower speed.

That means instead of getting whacked by the club that is going 30 mph, you're going to be running into his arm, which is only doing 5 mph.[6] In case you haven't figured it out yet, that'll hurt a whole lot less. Also, while you're up close, most people have no idea what to do with a distance weapon when they're suddenly nose to nose. Not only do their brains go "tilt" at the new situation, but the physics for an effective strike change dramatically. In fact, often it is impossible to muster a really effective strike with a distance weapon at close range. You have to have it in certain positions which you may be able to get to in time.

I once had a pool cue in hand when a guy pulled a knife on me at point-blank range. Instead of hitting him with the cue (which would have left me wide open) I dropped the cue and grabbed him. I hoisted him onto the table by a tender portion of his anatomy and started dribbling him across the pool table. Remember, whatever you do has to work in the time that it takes for the guy to recover. That's because he can do more damage faster with a weapon than you can with bare hands! *If his recovery time is faster than your put-down time, you're screwed!*

Okay, so now we've discussed all the basics of what's involved in neutralizing the threat. The term neutralize means exactly what it says—neither attacking nor running, merely holding in check for the moment. At this moment, you have to make a critical decision. Do you stay and fight, or do you bug out?

There are several factors involved in this decision. The major one is the answer to the question, "Is the fucker alone?" Scum runs in packs. Most of the time the answer is "No, the sucker's got back-up." I've said it before and I'll say it again: *If the guy doesn't think he can get away with it, he won't make a move in the first place.* These days, it either means the guy's got a weapon or some buddies that will help him out when it goes bad. It's not a one-on-one in most serious situations, so it's best to bug out.

Question number two: Are you alone? If you are, there is no reason why you should stay around. If the cards are stacked against you, fold your hand and go home. Alone, a bug-out is a pretty simple thing. However, when you're with someone else, he had better know how to attack and/or disappear when the time is right. Seven against two is not good odds— skeedaddle! In fact, it wouldn't hurt to loan this book to your running buddies so you all have the same ideas about rabbiting. (My publisher hates it when I say stuff like that. "No, Animal, have them *buy* it!" Okay, sell this book to your friends.)

The real hairball is when you are with your lady. Your running buddies may know how to react when trouble hits the fan, but unless it's been worked on before, I wouldn't bet that your old lady knows how. Women live in a different world than men. They think differently about certain situations than men do, and because of this they will react differently than you think they will. If you don't know about this before-hand, you both can get hurt.

Now, I have to tell you that recently I got into a heated discussion over this issue with a woman I really respect. In fact, hers is the only women's self-defense course that I actively support. She teaches a system that can wake up the the part that a person needs in order to survive combat. Her system works well when a lone woman is confronted with an attacker. Because of imagined superiority on the part of the attacker, a woman is less likely to be attacked by a weapon than a man. In this type of situation, there is no one better than my friend.

What bothers me is that there is an entirely different dynamic involved when a male and female are confronted together. Her point was that the female is just as capable of taking care of herself as a man in such a situation. Therefore, the woman shouldn't have to run while the man holds a rearguard action. Theoretically, I agree with her, but experience tells me different. It isn't a matter of what do I think when someone else is facing the situation; it's what the people involved think. Alone, either could take care of the situation, although the techniques would be different. When they are together, however, sociological patterns often take over. In this situation, techniques can—and often do—collide. Without joint training, couples end up tripping over each other when confronted on the streets.

Both parties need to know their individual limits and skills, as well as those of their partner. That comment doesn't even have anything to do with gender, but rather respect for each other's talents in certain areas. That means both parties need to know to back down and take the lead from the other in certain situations. This means trusting each other, folks.

Where this issue does go into the topic of gender is when either party feels that it's a gender issue. Up to that point it's just a matter of who's more experienced and able to deal with it. The one girlfriend I had who nearly got me killed the most was the one who didn't know when to back down. She felt that it was a horrible injustice for her to back down just because she was a woman. Technically, I agree, but not when my ass is on the line. She would look at a situation and, instead of accepting that I was more experienced and taking her cues from me, she felt that it was a matter of sexism and had to throw in her two cents.[7] A lot of unnecessary shit happened because she wouldn't ease off.

On the other hand, I had a New York Italian lover who was incredible to watch in action. This woman was so slick I took notes. There were times that I had to bite my cheek to keep from laughing, she was laying it out so fast. It wasn't because she was afraid of it getting ugly. To tell you the truth, though, that woman was nastier than I was when she got pissed. (This was the same woman who was safe as long as she was screaming, but when she got quiet and started speaking in Italian, I'd head for any hole big enough to pass as an exit.) She once calmly handed me a pool cue when I was facing someone. The thing to note here was when she was handling it, she was handling it; when I was, I was.

Honestly, though, as much as it may piss some women off, there are situations wherein, by the grace of gender, it is better to let a man handle the whole thing. If she wants to help, she can coach the guy in a low voice. Generally these sorts of situations revolve around certain ethnic groups and social levels wherein women are truly second-class citizens. Unless you are seriously cutting territories, though, these situations aren't as common as many people think. For the most part, the sex of who's handling it doesn't really matter; the skill and experience do.

There are situations where it's better to let a woman handle it.[8] I've seen shit blow up just as fast because a guy decided to step in to "handle" a situation. If you know you're a hothead and she's handling it well, let her do the talking. If you jump in too soon it can go to hell in a handbasket just as quick. If you see it actually going to pieces (as opposed to you just think you can handle it better), then step forward and tell her you're moving in. If it is really slipping out of control, she should have no problem with letting you come forward.

Guys, let's take a reality break here. Just because you have a dick doesn't mean that you are qualified to handle a situation that is turning violent. This belief is bullshit! Most people don't know how to fight regardless of their genitalia. In spite of this bit of reality, the mythos remains. Apparently, there exists in men an instinctive or conditioned reflex to protect women during a crisis. Unfortunately, this means most times you're so busy protecting the female that you don't protect yourself. That's why they keep women off the front lines in combat. It doesn't matter if they are conditioned or instinctive, these reflexes form a real behavior pattern for both men and women in our society. This becomes a problem is when the guy interprets it to mean that he *has* to become John Wayne in the face of violence.

Want to know a macho myth that women don't accept? It's the "Save yourself, Darling, while I fight a heroic rearguard action" myth. *If you say "run!" you do it too!* It is just as hard for a woman to run out on her man when he is in danger as it is for a man to split on her. Remember, if you're in the shit in the street, you've usually walked into an ambush. So you both need to get out of there.

This is what the self-defense lady and I were going round-robin about. She was insisting that there is no reason for the woman to run. My opinion is that culturally, most people are conditioned otherwise. To a point, this also includes myself. While I'd prefer to get the hell out of there, I'm not going to rabbit until I know she's clear. Call it sexism or whatever, that's just the way I'm wired, and I think most men are, too. Therefore, I'd consider it a great personal favor if the woman wouldn't argue about it. It's not that I'm going to valiantly hold off a horde of attackers, *it's that she's standing in the way of my retreat! I can't run until she does!*

I feel the problem with this is that women think guys are stupid in this area. Unfortunately, they have stable data to support this supposition. I had one even go so far as to ask me, "What makes you bulletproof?" The answer was, and still is, "I'm not." I just don't want someone I care about to take a slug. Silly me, I didn't realize that a woman might just feel the same way about me. (Of course, to a woman's way of thinking, what guys consider to be the most heroic act of love, she considers seriously dense.)[9]

Having seen more than a few examples of testosterone aggression, women aren't convinced that you're going to have the smarts to run when the shit gets ugly. Under those conditions, a woman will stay by your side. To avoid this little misunderstanding you have to tell her—and mean it—that you're going to be ducking and weaving right behind her. If she doesn't believe this, she ain't going nowhere. I tell you this from personal experience. Guys, women know that there's a difference between courage and ferocity; even the most timid lady will stick out her jaw and refuse to run if she thinks you're going to be facing the wrecking crew alone. Before she will boogie, she has to know that you're going to be with her when it's all over. It's no time for heroics; you both get the hell out of there. In fact, if you have a girlfriend, it wouldn't hurt for her to read this book too (do yourself a favor and don't try to sell it to her). That way, neither of you has to worry about the other doing something that will get you caught or hurt.

The bottom line of all of this is whoever is on point in a situation gives the bug-out orders. On the other hand, whoever is on back-up gives the "fall back" order. The difference? "Bug out" means to run. Fall back is where the point person steps back and reviews the situation. Often the point person becomes so wrapped up in the situation at hand that he/she cannot see peripheral stuff occurring, while the person behind can get a better overall picture. The back-up will often spot little things like a concealed knife or the opposite team surrounding you, while the point is too wrapped up in the face-off to notice. Once the point person is informed of the new development, he or she makes the choice to re-engage or bug out. If your back-up person is telling you to back up, you'd better listen. He or she may be seeing something you aren't.

The following works with everyone—your partner, your lover, your kin. It's Animal's Law of E & E Number 1: *When it's time to rock-and-roll, EVERYONE rock and rolls; when it's time to boogie, EVERYONE boogies!!!* You go in as a unit, you come out as one, bottom line. You don't run until you can all run! If you gotta carry, you do so! If someone isn't one of your own, you at least warn him, beyond a polite "get the fuck out of here," that he's on his own.

Question number three for the fight-or-flight decision: Are you cornered? Let me tell you, children, there will be times when the only way out of a situation is through the very person who has you cornered. You will notice I didn't say you had to fight the guy; I said *you have to go through him!* There is a world of difference between these two types of moves. One is where you stand there and slug it out, while the other is to dump him on his ass and split. Trying to fight your way out of a situation takes too long.

With the other way you're only in contact long enough to get past the obstruction. Contrary to popular belief, it's hard to keep a determined person from blowing by you. A determined 150 pounds slamming into anyone will give him pause. You get ahold of that person's stance integrity and he's going down. Just landing on their asses will slow down most folks, but if you can throw them into a bunch of trash cans it'll really complicate their day. Do it right and he goes down into a friend. That's how you take out two people at once. They're so busy trying to figure out whose elbow is up whose ass that they can't chase you.

It's my personal preference to take out the alpha (leader) and hurl his ass into his lieutenant. If you've just trashed the biggest dicks of the group, the guppies aren't going to be raring to come after you. That will give you time to stretch your lead. If you can't figure out who's who, just throw the guy who's doing the talking into the next-toughest-looking guy.

Important safety tip here, folks: *if you've just knocked the leader of a group on his ass, you still have to run!* In fact, you've just increased the need for the flat-foot floogie. Number one, he's down, not out. That means he's going to be getting up real soon now, and when he does, he's going to be pissed (that's number two)! Number three is you have just disrespected him in front of his followers, and now he has something to prove. If you are still around, he is going to use you as the object lesson as to why people don't do that to him.

On the other hand, if you're not there, it's likely the next person he's going to attack will be the group member who opens his mouth about the event. "Hey Joey, you really looked dumb sitting on your ass . . ." BLAM! Joey boy will have to reestablish his dominance that you so rudely undermined by planting him on his butt. As a passing thought, what you've made for life is *not* a friend. In fact, you've just made it to the top of Joey's most-wanted list for the next few months.

Not only do you have to be able to get away, but you'll
have to avoid him for a few months afterward. That's
where phase three of this book comes into play: the
fox-and-hound routine.

I'd like to point something out at this time that
could make this phase work much better for you,
especially if the guy's got a weapon. There's a big difference between fatal and incapacitating attacks. A
person can be incapacitated by an attack but not fatally wounded. The bad news is that someone can be
fatally wounded and not incapacitated for awhile.
He's mortally wounded, but the news hasn't gotten to
him yet. (Of course, if someone is really dead, he's
probably also incapacitated.)[10]

Eyes are great targets if the guy doesn't have a
knife. Whether bare-handed or armed with clubs or
even a gun, go for the eyes (but not if he has a knife; a
reflexive defensive action to protect his eyes will still
serve to slash you open). Remember, with a knife all
he has to do is touch you to hurt you. If he's got a gun,
taking his eyes out is a tits thing to do as you're running away. You don't have much to worry about from
a blind sniper, do you? (But like I said earlier, beyond
10 feet most people can't hit shit.)

Cutting off someone's air can supply hours of
entertainment, and it also effectively prevents pursuit.
There are two fast and effective targets to do this, the
throat and the diaphragm. I recommend you use the
throat shot in only the most extreme situations, as it
can be lethal. Your attacker's extended arm can be
used as a runway to his throat. Side-stepping a knife
thrust and winging a crane strike up the guy's arm
and into his throat is a motherin' fast move. While he's
dealing with a temporarily compressed throat, you're
beating feet. If you hit the guy hard enough it'll crush
his windpipe; however, the more common lethal
application happens as the guy's bruised windpipe

swells later and cuts off his air. If he's smart, he'll head for the hospital immediately, but often the guy will just go somewhere and pass out and later die. Be careful about whom you use this on, as amateurs will squeal to the cops and get both criminal and civil charges filed against you.

A safer move—from a legal standpoint, not necessarily for saving your ass—is an uppercut. The target of this blow is the diaphragm. An uppercut under the sternum not only paralyzes the diaphragm (hence the breathing process), but forces the reserve air out of the lungs. People normally keep a certain amount of air in their lungs when they exhale, so they don't feel like they're suffocating. If you've ever had the wind knocked out of you, you know how hard it is to breathe afterwards.

The bestest target of them all, from both a legal and incapacitating standpoint, is the knee. I don't care how big someone is. I don't care how bad someone is. A blown knee will take anyone down. If he ain't got two legs, he's not going to chase you very well, is he? Knees fold and bust better to the side than from straight on.[11] Also, if you gouge someone's eye out the courts will usually say that's worse than breaking someone's leg. If someone gets a broken leg while attacking someone else, it often gets a "tough shit" reaction from juries. On the other hand, blinding one eye evokes more of a knee-jerk reaction.

It helps to exit a situation with your possible pursuit back at ground zero struggling with being incapacitated. Failing to achieve this preferred state, the next best thing is to leave one or two of them sitting on their butts while you're legging it out of there. This now takes us to phase two of *Street E & E*: the hot pursuit!

Notes

1. A few years ago, I had this delusion that I had said everything about violence that I had to say in one book. Boy was I wrong.

2. For clarity's sake, I've changed the identification system to A, B, C, D, instead of the original numbers.

3. Which is why the Submarine Corps and UDTs are not much liked by the rest of the navy. They sit around and think up ways to sink boats. Wonderful way to stay popular with your friends in boats. I watched one of these conversations between a former UDT and PBR (Patrol Boat River). The UDT guy was the PBR's worst nightmare as he happily explained ways he had sunk boats.

4. In my video *Surviving a Street Knife Fight*, I made a big distinction between an effective and correct attack. The odds are seriously against someone who is not actually trained in knife fighting making a correct attack. Even if the guy has carried a blade for years.

5. Throwing doesn't count because it's nearly impossible to hit a moving target. You may knock him out by having the butt hit him in the head, but when it comes to sticking, forget it.

6. By the way, I just made those numbers up. If anyone is good at math (which I am not), what would be the top speed of a 2-foot-long club at arm's length? Feel free to use your own arm measurement.

7. The time that I was facing off a 51-50, sexism had nothing to do with it. All I was concerned about was making sure Senior Psycho didn't go off on me, and she was pissing him off further.

8. I know of one situation where a drug freak-out with a knife had a group of guys surrounding him. A woman who had been skinny dipping over by the river came running up. The freak-out turned at her and waved the knife at her and screamed, "Do you want

this?!" She calmly reached out her open hand and said, "Yes." The guy looked at her and handed her the knife. Boom—situation resolved. It turned out she was a therapist. Something police have found out is that violence is less likely to happen if a female cop is present.

9. But if you really want to show how much you care for her, flowers work much better than getting shot.

10. Also, if you incapacitate him, it's hard to prove you were trying to kill him. Remember, especially if you call the police, scum will try to sue you even though they started it. While there's a certain ruthlessness about it, there's much less paperwork if you drop a body in a Dumpster. If it weren't for this tendency of the legal profession to represent scum in this manner, I wouldn't have to say this. If you object to this situation (as I do) write your local legislator to get laws like Colorado, Arizona, and Nevada have. These laws basically say if someone is hurt while committing a crime, tough shit.

11. *Fists, Wits, and a Wicked Right* goes into this sort of stuff extensively.

CHAPTER THREE

Hasta la Vista, Baby!

> "The few are those on the defensive against others; the many are those who cause others to be on the defensive against themselves."
>
> —Sun Tzu
> *The Art of War*

I was minding my own business, lying under a truck, while a pack of surfers was running through an open apartment gate. The gate was swinging as if someone who looked incredibly like me had just run through it mere moments ago. After I was convinced that the oil filter on the truck didn't need replacing—coincidentally, at the same time that the last of the four guys disappeared—I rolled out from under that truck and hotfooted it down the way that we'd all just come from.

Three minutes later I was as many blocks over and considerably farther west. While I can't be certain, I figure it was about the same time that the rocket scientists realized that I had given them the slip. All of this over my retaliation for their trying to drown me during Aquatics class. Their friend, whom I had caught alone, would be out of a cast in a few weeks, so what was their problem? Some people can dish it out, but they can't take it.

This episode occurred during one of the most fucked periods of my life, when I was being hunted by a clique of the Venice surfers. I got along with all the Venice homeboys, esés, Bloods, pachucos, and assorted charmers. Oddly enough, it was with a pack of suntanned white trash that I had the most problems. This was before the term "surf Nazis" came into vogue, but these guys weren't far from it. Gosh, yours truly didn't have blond hair, blue eyes, and a surfboard whose length was more than my IQ; so I was a target.

The real problem was that I was outnumbered, severely. The game was they would try to catch me when I was alone, and I would catch them when one of them was alone. Unlike today with the pscyho gangsters, when either side was surrounded by people the game was off. At the end the score was two to one. I'd caught two of them alone and been nailed with a hit-and-run strike by one of their members (the very asshole who had started it, coincidentally). However, there had been more than a few incidents of my having to evaporate at a moment's notice often to the shattering of beer bottles and the roaring of engines. (I never could get them to crash that damn car, though.)

Hot pursuit is more than just running like a bat out of hell. Several things can affect your getting out of there in a hurry: if you aren't in the best of shape, if there's more of them than you, if you're out of your territory and in theirs, if they have radios (you bad boy), or if the other team is in vehicles. Of course, a helicopter can really fuck things up, but that's an extreme case. By the way, if you're going to be pursued by helicopters, there are some tricks you should know. Light does weird things from up above. One of the main things it does is reflect footprints in the dew on grass. If you're leaving a scene where the cops will show up with a helicopter, stay off the grass as much as possible. The length of stride from a running person is greater than that of a walker. If they see that, they know which way you were headed. Every time they get a solid clue as to where you're heading, they narrow down where you are.

The best place to lose a helicopter pursuit if you're on foot is in the rain drainage system. There is a problem, however. That means you need to know either where there are holes big enough to crawl into or carry one of those metal rods that city maintenance guys carry to lift manhole covers. (Not real likely, that last one, except in your car.)

First of all, there are two kinds of pursuit. One is they are just doggin' you. They're following you (at high speed) just for the fun of watching you run. After they've run you out of their territory, they're going to swagger back to home base and pee on a tree. They may even scratch the dirt with their back legs. If you've ever seen a dog run another out of its territory, you know what is going on. To get out of this situation, all you have to do is run outside their territorial boundaries. An amazing thing happens—miraculously they always seem to get bored with chasing someone right as they approach the edge of their turf. (Of course, they'd never admit that's why they quit chasing you.)

Most teenage pursuits are this kind. Someone will be walking by a party, and the next thing you know there's a pack of guys thundering after you. Always check six (look behind you) after you pass an idle group for this very reason. Give it about a hundred feet and then check again at two hundred. Also, listen for the pounding of many tiny feet or any cars suddenly peeling out behind you. You can be chased by people in vehicles just as easily as on foot.

I've had to haul ass out of a few places for just being in the wrong place at the wrong time. When you're young, drunk, and not likely to get laid that night, chasing a total stranger down the street seems like the next best thing. If someone is too lazy to actually give chase, jumping in the car and throwing beer bottles at someone is also acceptable.

If an unexplained car comes tearing up the road, either ghost into a shadow or duck behind a car before the headlights hit where you are standing. The advantage to being chased by people in a car is that the headlights mess up their night vision. If you're out of the headlights and you're moving slowly, it's hard to spot you. Of course, cop cars have search lights, so it's a different story. I'll go into dodging cars later.

Pursuits are more common at night but can occur in daylight if you come too close to a special hangout. If you know that a group of rowdies hangs out at a certain place, don't go there. That's the best way to avoid being chased. In case you're wondering how you can tell if it's a hangout, it's really rather simple. If there's a large pack of guys who all look vaguely alike standing around with no real reason to be there, it's probably a hangout. Alleys, parks, empty parking lots, front yards, and jetties aren't normally the hub of social interaction or legal commerce. Most legit businesses don't want a wolf pack hanging around and will shoo the guys away. This is standard operating procedure, unless the pack spends enough money to make up for the customers that it's scared away. Most teenagers don't have that kind of money.

Although it is hard to believe while you're running for all you're worth, these sorts of pursuits are the least dangerous. If they catch you they'll maul you, but fundamentally, their hearts aren't into it. If it gets too complicated or you have too much of a lead, they usually give up quickly. They soon lose interest and go back to such exciting pastimes as drinking, belching, spitting, seeing who can pee the farthest, and wondering why girls want nothing to do with them.

Hot pursuit, however, is a different matter altogether. This is when someone is after you and isn't likely to blow it off without a major reason. If you have just dropped one of their own, happen to have aroused their ire, are the featured guest at an assault, or whatever, they aren't going to give it up so quickly. In fact, most times you have to persuade them to back off.

Surviving a hot pursuit is a unique combination of messing up your pursuers via confusion, obstacles, counterattacks, hiding, and my all-time favorite tool, their own stupidity. Basically, the best way to be safe during a hot pursuit is to make it real risky to get too close to you. Sooner or later the other side is going to realize that every time they get close to you, you get a piece out of them; not, as they had hoped, the other way around. When this begins to sink into their heads, they are going to slow down. When they slow down, you begin to confuse them. During this confusion is when you slip away.

Hot pursuit usually starts in one of four places or situations: 1) the scene of a face-off where someone is now sitting on his ass gasping for breath; 2) the scene of a face-off where everyone is still on their feet; 3) out in the open where a fan club has caught you and sent you bolting for cover; 4) a surprise meeting where you have accidently run into each other (while not particularly flattering, this one happens a lot). Each of these situations has a different psychology. The reason this psychology is important is that it will affect how seriously they will come after you.

In the first case, they're sort of shocked that you've managed to put one of their own down. Everyone on their team was hyped for it to go another way, but the situation is now something unexpected that's going to put them off stride. As these people pursue you, they will know that you are capable of getting a piece out of them. The bulk of the people may either stay with the downed person, or if they do pursue they're going to be thinking seriously about whether chasing you is worth a piece of their own ass. People in this state of mind are usually going to back off much more quickly than anyone else, especially if you're pulling rearguard actions that pop up unexpectedly. On the other hand, you and yours are eminently aware of the trouble and are psyched for it. This gives you an edge.

The second type of situation is one where your pursuers have no idea that you're capable of hurting them. These guys are the hardest to shake. Until they learn differently, they are going to be committed to the chase. In all chases, your pursuers are likely to string out. If your rearguard actions take out the third or fourth person in the string, the people behind him will slow down, but the ones in front will keep on coming on strong. In situations like this, you have to show everyone that chasing you is not a smart move. You have to aim at the guys who are in the lead. Your psychology is going to be that you've had time to prepare for the chase during the face-off. Here, as in the first case, you're going to be psyched for what you are going to have to do.

Now I must warn you—there are times when even if you're in a number 1, you can still get a retardo or two who will be in the mind-set of number 2. They don't care that you took down ol' Billy Bob; they're going to hurt you anyway. Aggressive, stupid, and

54

mean (ASM) is not the best way to stay alive a long time against a cagey opponent. In any pursuit, the mean ones are your main enemies. Fortunately, in situations like this, most of the pack is still in the mind-set of number 1, with ASM being the only one committed to pursuit. The rest will be giving up soon. The one or two ASMs are your targets!

The number three scenario is by far the worst. Your opponents have had time to spot you and psych themselves up. The fact that they are running after you means that they have had time to work themselves up into a frenzy, one that you have to shake them from. You, on the other hand, are starting out cold. Your first hint of trouble is to look up and see a horde swooping down on you. Not one, not two, but a thunderin' herd of ASMs. Your first reaction is to bolt (good reaction). From a standing start, you must go to a pure flight, then, as quickly as possible, to a rearguard action. Going from trying to shake catsup onto your fries to dragging trash cans in front of your pursuers is a mighty big jump to make in three seconds. Unfortunately, unless you want to be doing the emergency room shuffle, you'd better be able to make it.

As I said, scenario number 4 is more common than you'd believe. That's where you turn the corner and you and the Glee Club are suddenly nose to nose. Oops! The advantage is that both of you are starting from ground zero. They haven't worked their way up to a full frenzy and are as surprised as you. If you immediately bolt, they have nothing to stop them from escalating into full-pursuit mode. The trick is to discourage them, either immediately, by turning it into a number 1 (i.e., you deck one of them and run like hell), or by dropping little hints in their way (like trash cans) within moments of the pursuit's start.

The reason this is important is that someone who is in an unchecked frenzied state isn't going to catch on that his ass is in danger as quickly as someone who's more calm. You have to tell these people that chasing you can and will be harmful to their health. Once this message gets through to them, then they begin to slow down. Once they slow down, you begin to have room to maneuver.

How gonzo someone is about chasing you will determine how slow he is to get the message.[1] In a group, there are generally only going to be one or two people who really have a hard-on for you. If I feel that you were the guy who set me up, I'm going to be much more determined to catch you than my buddy who's only tagging along because I've got a hard-on with you. Even if there is a faster runner in the group, it's the guy who's got the boner with you who's going to be the hardest to shake. If you start dropping stuff in your path, the lesser-committed guys are going to slow down.

While the most preferred course of action is dragging stuff into your pursuers' way, a more likely event is taking them through an obstacle course. There won't always be trash cans, pallets, and winos to throw into your pursuers' faces so you have to make it up as you go along. This includes bouncing over fences, hedges, cars, and walls; around trees; over people lying in the park or beach, etc. Anytime you make it more difficult for your pursuers to continue after you, you've achieved one of your main goals, which is to make them string out.

And that brings us to Animal's Law of E & E Number 2: *It's easier to ditch people if your pursuers are strung out behind you.* When a group has begun to string out, the people at the end are more likely to give up pursuit than the guys in the front. Not only are they slower runners, but they are usually less committed. The harder a course you set, the more strung out the group is going to get. In case you didn't know, it's easy to jack-rabbit over a fence alone. However, going over that same fence with three other guys slows you all down. Not only is it wiggling and bouncing, but you have to worry about getting kicked in the head by your buddy. If you bolt through a hedge, someone is likely to trip while going through it. If you clear a jump, someone behind is going to either not clear it or decide that it's too much work to keep after you. If you've practiced clearing the wall, the odds are that someone behind you hasn't. His time over the wall will be slower than yours.

Now let's cover a very important aspect of E & E, dogs. When I was a young buck, I nearly left my nuts on a fence because I was exiting a place quickly. The cops had come in the front door and I was in the backyard. Truth be told, they were just busting a party, but I was in serious pocket and not about to throw that much money away. I rabbited across the yard and went over the fence. As I reached the top of the fence, Rover hit the other side. Did I ever mention that anytime you're looking down the maw of an attacking animal it's a saber-toothed? So there I was, looking down at a saber-toothed dog, and I decided that maybe I didn't really want to go that way. An interesting point of physics here: unless worked upon by another force, gravity works. I was halfway over the fence with one leg going over when I arrested my forward action. No forward action, gravity takes over. Owwww! The cops didn't see me because I was lying in the bushes, whimpering.

The reason that happened was because I was in a strange neighborhood. In your own home area (or along a route you normally walk), know where all the dogs are. That way if you have to skidoo, you don't jump into Rover's water dish, thereby irritating Rover. In cases like that, the bad guys who were chasing you will just hang out on the fence, watching you get mauled.

Now an interesting trick that my first stepdad did was to find the nastiest, most vicious dog in the neighborhood and start feeding it. Eventually, he became friends with Killer. Thereafter, when the bad guys were chasing him, he'd zip through the yard and toss the dog a marshmallow. The dog also got to eat anyone who followed my stepdad into the yard. Once that barrier came up, then he'd give the bad guys the slip.

The object is to buy space between you and your pursuers. Unless you're Speed Racer, you want to avoid open areas. In the open, you're simply outrunning them, which, if you can do it, is fine. The more daring a course you can lay, the more likely your pursuers are to either give up on their own or get hurt and then give up. The nastier the moves, the faster they'll lay off you.

Now, before I go on, I want to make something very clear here. Right here, right now, let me say, *Don't use physically damaging techniques on a cop!* Running is bad enough, but if you hurt one, you're in deep shit. What bozos don't understand is there are limits to how far you can push a cop, anyway. The reality of the situation is 99 times out of a hundred if someone gets mauled by a cop he's done something to deserve it! If you peel away all the rhetoric and brouhaha that you hear on TV, this simple fact remains: *cops don't pound on someone for no reason!* This starts at lipping off to them and progresses from there.

Despite the bad press the Los Angeles Police Department (LAPD) got over the Rodney King incident, that they whaled on him is 100-percent understandable. A high-speed chase, a 20-minute confrontation, two Tasers, and refusal to stay down on the ground, and you got yourself a solid stomping. In the heat of the moment, civil rights don't exist, adrenaline does. I'm not saying the cops were right in what they did. I am, however, saying that given what happened, you should be about as shocked by the sun rising as by that beating happening.

Anyone who is hung up on the idea that cops shouldn't react like this is living in fantasy land! There is a *beaucoup* difference between policy and reality. Cops are people, and they have their limits too. It always amazes me that criminals who make their livelihood breaking the rules of the game get so bent out of shape when the cops do the same. I'm talking a tantrum that would do credit to a 3-year-old. I mean, how many years of therapy does it take to get to the place where you're the only one who can break the rules? What kind of double standard is it that only you get to back-stab, shoot, beat, and set people up, but nobody can do it to you? It's like the guy who kidnapped and raped a woman who said, "Yeah I did it, but you shouldn't be too hard on me." Bullshit!

Animal's Law of E & E Number 3: *If you run from a cop, make sure you get away, because it's going to go hard on you if you don't!* Use that as the deciding factor to run or not.

It is illegal to run from a cop in the first place, so if you make it too hard on them they are going to hurt you when they catch you. The American Civil Liberties Union (ACLU) can snivel, whine, and sue as much as they want, but it is a basic human reaction when you play predator/prey games. You've already set the game rules by running. If they catch you, they may tear you up anyway. But if you do anything but go totally passive when they catch you it's guaranteed you're going to get hurt. If you hurt one on the way, you may not live through it. Something I know about cops is once they get the "ON" button pushed they have a hard time stopping. I wouldn't wish a cop's job on my worst enemy. They are exposed to the absolute worst aspect of humanity day in and day out. They have a job where somebody is always going to be pissed at them no matter what they do. The judicial system they serve is fucked-up beyond all repair. They are constantly exposed to death, whether it's from homicide, suicide, car wreck, or natural causes. Worst of all, their best efforts amount to trying to bail the ocean out with a bucket. All in all, they have a job that would have the most bleeding-heart liberal saying, "Kill 'em all; let God sort 'em out" in a month.

With this in mind, I want you to think about what your reaction would be to this situation. After being drowned in bullshit, negativity, and frustration day in and day out, where you constantly see dead bodies so you have no illusions as to your immortality, some loud-mouthed motherfucker rabbits on you. That first moment of "Oh shit, is he going to kill me?" has now been replaced with "This asshole is running!" Suddenly that rabbit is the target of every bit of frustration, suppressed anger, and paranoia that you have. When you catch Speed Racer, how compassionate are you going to be?

This is why I seriously don't recommend running from cops. Even if, after pursuit, you go totally limp when he touches you as a sign of submission, you still might get hurt. If this happens, it will be nobody's fault but your own. If you can't run with the big dogs, stay on the porch. If you rabbit from a cop and then get uppity when you're caught, don't be surprised if you get treated like a King. . . .

Let's get back to the Zen of E & E. Well, I'm going to do what Zen doesn't and spell it out for you. There are a few basic factors involved in street E & E: 1) you don't want to get caught; 2) you want them to quit chasing you; and 3) if possible, you want to discourage them from the idea that this is fun and they might want to do it again in the future.

I divide the first two for a very simple reason. You can run all day and not get caught. Unfortunately, your pursuers will have no reason to stop chasing you. It's during the second section that most people blow it. Remember, the idea is evade and escape.

The not getting caught part is a fundamental aspect. As long as nobody has a hold on you or has nailed you with a beer bottle, you ain't caught. The chase ain't over, but you ain't caught either. Getting caught can come about in many different ways. In fact there are many subfactors that one must take into consideration to prevent it, which we will cover in a bit. The main thing to remember in this is the "evade" aspect.

The next step is you want them to quit chasing you. This is the "escape" aspect. This is also where most people screw the pooch and end up getting caught. A simple mistake here can eat up any slack you've bought and get you caught. Failing to divide these two aspects, many people try to escape while they should still be concentrating on evasion! Most people do something to end the pursuit, but they do it too soon! Without the slack that evasion has bought you, trying to escape will, more often than not, result only in your getting caught!

Let us take a look at a rather innocent item, a wall. We'll make it brick and about 6 feet high. As long as you are running alongside of it, there is little chance that it will slow you down. However, if you happen to turn and attempt to scale this wall, you will discover something rather important. *It is slower to clear an item than it is to run on flat ground!* Take this to heart, people, because it's where most folks fuck up! They think they're going to shake their pursuers, and they do exactly what it is that gets them caught! They slow down at the wrong time!

Animal's Law of E & E Number 4: *Don't try to go over something that will slow you down if your pursuers are closer than 50 feet!* There is a sliding scale of height, your ground speed, obstacle clearance time, and pursuers' ground speed to consider. A good rule of thumb is, the higher something is, the longer it takes to clear. It's the old story problem: "If Bob and Jack are so far apart and traveling at such-and-such a speed, where will they meet?" How fast is that guy going to be able to close the distance? If it's faster than you can get over something, you're screwed. The higher or more difficult the object is to clear, the longer lead space you'll need. An 18-foot fence takes a good 50-yard lead to clear safely. It's important to remember your pursuer doesn't have to clear the object. All he has to do is leap high enough to grab you and drag your ass back down!

When I was a young buck in Venice, the esés had the art of fence-popping down pat. Nobody could clear a fence like the pachucos. You'd see literally a dozen of them swarm over a fence in a hot New York second. It was nearly a precision drill team, these guys were so good. They'd hit the fence, pivot over with their legs in the air, and land running. Naturally, I buzzed my homeboy Trini as to the art. He taught me how to do it, but it was practice that made it work.

Where most people goof when it comes to clearing objects is they don't practice enough when they aren't being pursued to be any good at it when they are. I have seen more poor schmucks run face-first into a wall at high speed than I care to remember (as has anyone who has been on a military obstacle course). The reason people plow into walls is very simple. They're trying to do a right-angle turn to get over the wall.

Look real close at that diagram, because that's how most people try to go over a wall. There are four right-angle changes in that line of force before it returns to its original course. First and foremost, the most common reaction to that sort of scenario is the guy is going to plow into the wall face-first. Face it, kinetic energy doesn't like to make 90-degree

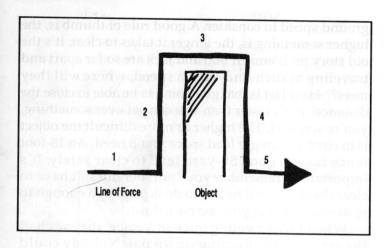

Wall and five lines of force.

turns. It gets cranky when you try to force it to do so. You're more likely to get about a foot off the ground before you realize that 90 degrees is too much to expect and—surprise, surprise—it ain't going to happen. Usually you're doing between 15 and 20 mph when you realize this. What was that quote? "Hell is truth realized too late?" BAM! You kiss the wall, then your buddies start doing the masochism tango on your head!

Another fun thing is that even if you don't kiss the wall, you seriously lose time. The reason is your line of force must actually stop, turn, start up again, peter out enough to turn again, and/or be boosted to that turning point, stop, turn again, and proceed along a parallel line to your original course. Then maybe you can let gravity take over. Yeah, right! The homeboys caught your ass in the middle of the third step. You lose too much time doing it that way. This is why a shitload of people are nailed on fences and walls. Hell, even Hollywood gets it right now and then, and you'll see someone on TV get nailed on the fence.

The secret of what my homeboy Trini taught me was that you didn't climb a fence, you ran over it! It isn't that you merely jump up into the air to change your approach vector to 45 degrees. While it's the right general idea, that would only mean slamming

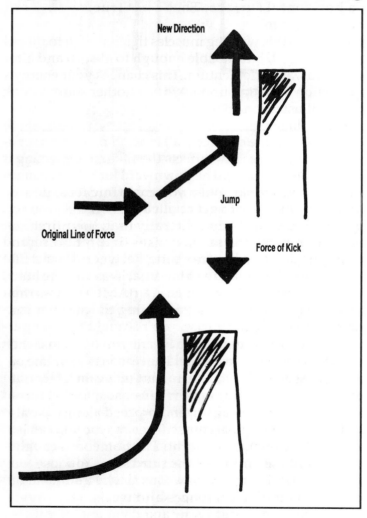

Running over a wall.

into the wall higher up. What you do is extend a leg out. When your foot connects you begin to kick straight down toward the ground. You are literally jumping up from a vertical surface from the ball of your foot. Most of us think you can only jump up from a horizontal surface. That's not true, as any rock climber can tell you.

You do this with leg muscles tight enough to propel you upward, but flexible enough to absorb and alter your forward momentum. This changes your energy's direction by acting upon it from another source. Look at the illustration on the left.

The illustration shows a segmented process where the original line of force (LF) is acted on by two separate events. The jump affects the LF first, deflecting it to a 45-degree angle. The downward kick then changes the LF to vertical. With minimal time loss, you've altered your LF but never stalled it.

Now the next step is literally that. Your first foot contact took you so high; now it's time for the second one. Incidentally, it works better on fences if your first foot hits ball-first and not toe-first. If you do the latter, you're likely to either wedge your toe too far in so you can't get it out or bounce off a wire and lose your traction entirely. In either case, you're caught by your pursuers. You can use the extra leverage of a toe wedge on your second step, but avoid it on the first.

The reason you can use a toe wedge on the second step is that your forward motion has been arrested (oohh, bad choice of words), so your toe isn't likely to get. Furthermore, by that time you're going to need the extra leverage and traction that a toe wedge offers. Unless you got some sort of supershoes that can hang onto vertical surfaces, your traction is going to start getting a little hinky around this time.

Another important issue about getting over a fence is that until you reach the top, you're crunched up in a

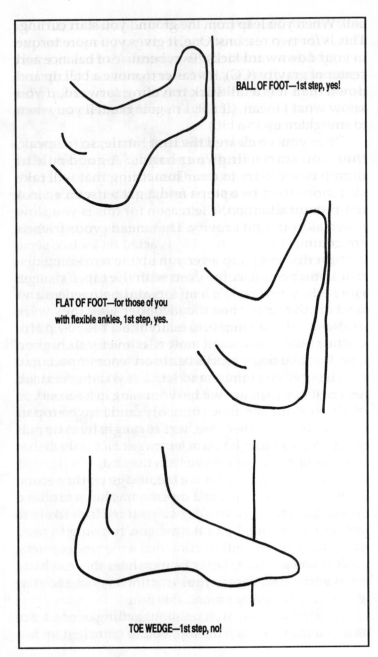

BALL OF FOOT—1st step, yes!

FLAT OF FOOT—for those of you
with flexible ankles, 1st step, yes.

TOE WEDGE—1st step, no!

ball. When you leap from the ground you start curling. This is for two reasons. One, it gives you more torque in your downward kicks. Two, because of balance and center of gravity (CG), it's easier to move a ball up and down than it is a tall stick traveling forward, if you know what I mean. (If not, I'm going to tell you when to straighten up in a bit.)

Once you've cleared the first hurtle, so to speak, then you start using your hands. A good rule of thumb is not to try to clear something that will take you more than two steps and a grab if you're in a hot-pursuit situation. The reason for this is you slow down as you fight gravity. That means your friends are getting closer.

Your first grab is to lever you up the remaining distance you need to come even with the top. I've seen more than a few people leap forward onto fences and land on all fours. Then they wonder why they were dragged off the fence and beaten to a bloody pulp. Without the downward action to lever you higher, limbs are just pogo sticks that absorb your impact onto the surface. The other hand has a real important job ahead of it, which we will be discussing in a second.

By this time, you've probably come to the top of an 8-foot fence. Here's where it gets interesting. If you try to straddle it you're screwed. Not only is that the slowest way to go over a fence, but it's the one most likely to get you mauled on the pointy ends. There's another really good reason not to straddle a fence. Your buddies will be hitting it any time now. If you're straddling it and they shake you loose, guess what you can kiss off?

It took me until I was in gymnastics in school before I became comfortable with what I'm about to tell you. On the other hand, this is how the esés did it all the time. Not only is it fast and flamboyant, but it is also somewhat risky. Then again, so is getting stomped by four or five guys, so you have to make your own decisions.[2]

What Trini taught me was to basically shoot beyond the top of the fence. It wasn't until my center of gravity was past the fence top that I began to go over. Now I never could do it like Trini, who would rocket up and flip over the fence with his body held straight. I used to go over in a ball. You need to figure out what works best for you. Your body's center of gravity is somewhere around your navel. That is what you have to get over the fence. Wherever the CG is, everything else follows. The trick is to get

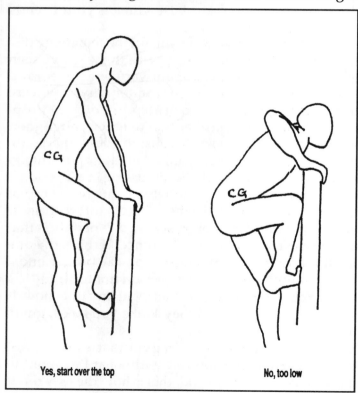

Yes, start over the top   No, too low

Clearance.

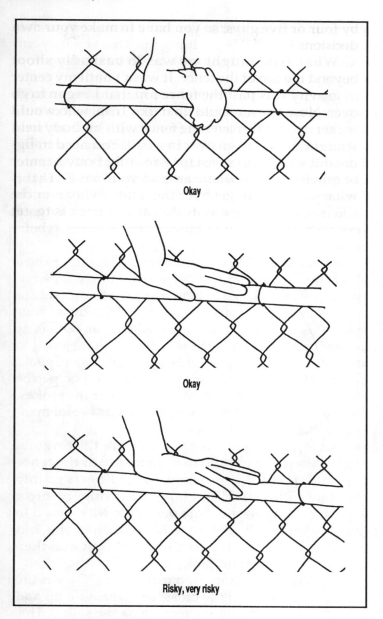

Okay

Okay

Risky, very risky

Hand grips.

everything else over at the same time or in such a manner that it won't get hung up. This is why your CG has to be either level with or above the fence top before you go over.

Remember that free hand you had floating around a second ago? It's not free anymore. Believe it or not, it's easier to go over a fence from the inside than from the outside. The reason for this is that there is a cross-bar which steadies the fence.[3] Above that crossbar are the chopped-off barbs of the top of the fence. From the inside you can put your hand on that crossbar much more easily. From the outside you have to navigate around the barbs to get hand placement, which is both more difficult and riskier.

However you grab that crossbar, there has to be a direct line of support from your palm into your wrist and forearm. Be careful about using the thumb side of your palm, as that makes it easier to slip and lose your grip. This is because you can't wedge your hand in as far with your thumb in the way. Since you're going to be holding your body weight on this hand soon, you'd better believe that's important. This arm is going to be used as the fulcrum for your pivot over the spikes. That's why it has to be placed in the most solid manner available.

Disengaging your other arm from the original grab, you reach over to the other side of the fence and latch on further down. All your fingers go into one fence diamond. You hook your fingers into a claw and keep your thumb out of the way. I used to bunch all of my fingers together into one point, but many people use all four fingers at first and then pull out the index and pinky.

From this position, you pull your CG over the fence. Your hand on the crossbar levers you up and prevents you from getting torn up on the spikes. This is the point where it becomes a matter of upper body strength. You must adjust your arms and legs for leverage and torque required to get you over the fence.

It is at this point that you will discover why you don't want your fingers enmeshed in the fence at more than one spot. Real soon that one spot is going to become a pivot point. If you have your fingers and

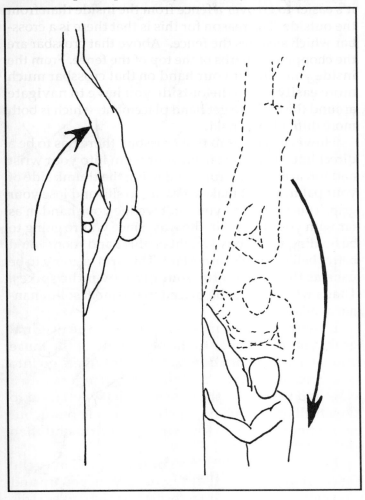

Olympic dismount.

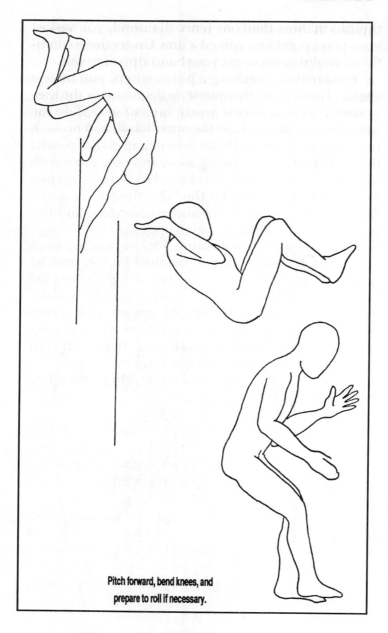

Pitch forward, bend knees, and
prepare to roll if necessary.

Olympic dismount.

thumbs in more than one fence diamond, you've lost your pivot point and gained a line. Under these conditions, you're going to get your hand ripped to shit.

You are now reaching a point where you have a choice. That is, the Olympic-style dismount or the less-graceful tumble. No esé worth his salt would do the tumbling dismount. I, on the other hand, had no such reservations. Trini would lever over and do a flip-twist that left him standing facing away from the fence with his pivot hand still enmeshed. Fucking gorgeous move. In fact, I dubbed it the "Olympic dismount." The difference between me and my Mexican buddies is they had a standard of cool to uphold.

I, on the other hand, being a *huero*, had no such standards. I would continue the flip I had started, let go of the fence, and land on my feet. If I was going too fast or off-balance, I'd just drop into a tumble. Remember me and gymnastics? I was young and lithe back then, and I could do a forward roll and pop up running with no problem. You have to figure out your own style to get over a fence quickly.

However you choose to do this, there are a few things I should point out.

1) *Some people prefer to go over between the upright poles because the mesh is more flexible and the play acts a shock absorber.* Personally, I prefer to go over near a pole, as it's more stable. Your choice. Experiment and decide for yourself.

2) *Go out and practice popping fences and walls.* This way you will know in advance which is a good height for you. If you can clear an 8-foot fence as fast as you can a 6-footer, you're going to shake more pursuers. On the other hand, if an 8-footer slows you down, don't risk it when you're hightailing it out of there.

3) *Clothing has a habit of getting snagged in fence tops.* Especially bulky winter clothes. Your clothes aren't

designed to hang from you upside down or in any of the other interesting positions you're going to find yourself in when going over a fence. This is part of why you need to clear the fence top with as much room as possible. Your arm on the crossbar is what will be holding you up high enough to keep you from getting snagged.

4) *Chain-link fences are not walls, wooden fences, or barbed wire.* Each of these reacts differently to a body going over it. Walls are not as flexible as chain-link, so your legs have to absorb more of the impact. Hitting an old, rickety wooden fence from the inside is risky, as you can kick out slats and, if not slam into the fence, get your foot caught. Try for the more solid objects if possible.

5) *Low fences and walls should be vaulted rather than jumped.* Unless you have track experience in running the hurdles, that kind of jump is likely to trip you up and leave you on your face. One-handed vaulting requires less energy and is more reliable. When you clear a fence, put your hand near a post, as it is more stable. If you jump, make sure you know what height you can clear before you try it in pursuit (especially with low fences without crossbars, as they will snag trailing pant legs).

6) *If you can't see the other side of the wall or fence, go far.* There may be things piled up against it. This is why I used to tumble over fences rather than the way Trini did it. I made sure I cleared whatever was on the other side. The big exception to this is parking lots. If you're vaulting into a parking lot, you're likely to twist your ankle on those concrete tire bumpers if you shoot out too far.

7) *Expect to tumble at any time when landing.* There are times that doing a quick tumble is faster and safer than trying to stay on your feet. If you bounce down and discover yourself heading for a stack of pallets, diving to the side and tumbling is a better bet than

slamming into them. You then spring up and keep on running. The guys behind you are likely to smash themselves up on that same obstruction.

8) *Shoot for the gap with hedges.* Every hedge consists of separate plants, and there are often gaps that are easier to run through than leap over. Shoot through them sideways and keep running. More than likely a few of the rah-rah club will get snagged up trying to jump or plow through the wrong place.

9) *If you know an area well and there are items that are hard to see in the dark, head for them.* A low wire fence, a ditch, a hole, or whatever is usually good for tripping up one or two pursuers. If you're not sure where a fence line is, run diagonally along its course until you find it. Then clear it and head off straight away from it. Those guys who are behind you will adjust course and head directly for the obstructions. You're more likely to see a fence running diagonally in its direction than you are heading directly at it. The same rule applies to your pursuers but is not to their advantage.

10) *It is my personal preference to go over backyard fences at the corners where four yards intersect.* If there's a dog or a cactus patch waiting on the other side, you still have two other options and no time lost.

In a similar vein, jumping is slower than running. If you're flapping away in the air, you're actually losing speed. If you weren't, you'd never touch down. It is also very difficult to land from a jump without losing more speed. Your feet hit the ground, and they want to stay there. By keeping your feet moving, you compensate for this resistance and keep on going. Unfortunately, due to the laws of physics we all have to abide by, you've already lost speed. The speed loss on first contact is more than the speed lost in the air. This is why you'll often see the second jumper tackle the first guy who jumped.

If, however, your feet are always on the ground, chugging along, you don't lose speed. If the guy is within 10 feet of you, don't jump. Ten feet sounds like a lot, but if you're doing 10 mph after ground contact and he's doing 20 in the air, how fast can he make up that 10-foot difference? (The answer is PDQ, pretty damn quick.)

The real trick to all of this is to go down to the local college track and do some practice. There is the long jump pit. First, how far can you jump? If you need to go over rooftops, this is an important thing to know. If you clear a 7-foot gorge, I guarantee you're going to slow down a few of your pursuers. Their little shoes will leave skid marks on the roof as they stop and say, "NOT!" If one of them happens to go splat, that will really take their minds off chasing you.[4]

The next question is, how far can you jump and still remain on your feet? You can long jump like a kangaroo and not be able to keep your feet under you. In case you haven't noticed, when you long jump you usually end up on your ass. Your effective jumping distance is what you can do and still stay upright and running. This is a serious thing to consider before you try doing a group jog.

The next question is, are you a sprinter or a distance runner? I'll tell you the truth—I was a shitty sprinter. I would get dusted in the 50- and 100-yard dashes. On the other hand, I'd be waving bye-bye to those same guys in the 880. My little cardiovascular system was going chug-chug-chug, while the sprinters were dying. This is what you need to know. If you're a sprinter, you need to do something fast to discourage your pursuers because you're going to be running out of steam real quick. Either you haul ass to a safe house, or you bug out and ditch your pursuers quick.

If you're a distance runner, you need to haul ass out

of the range of any sprinters in the group right quick. Many people can sprint, but their dicks go limp over the long run. If you've got distance running under your belt, make sure you get a good head start on your pursuers. Even if they have sprinters, a solid lead will outlast their wind. Of course, if someone gets too close, drop something in his way.

In either case, look into correct running form. There are books about jogging and running. Believe it or not, there are correct ways to run that will make you faster by conserving your energy. During the summer—or year-round in the warmer climes—there are marathon runs. These people know how to run. Go ask them how. I know a 55-year-old guy who is poetry in motion when he runs. He's got 20 years on me, and I couldn't catch him if my life depended on it. Why? He knows how to run correctly.[5]

The next track-related question is, how high can you jump? If you can only clear 3 feet, an attempt at a 4-foot jump is not going to turn out the way you want. In many situations, a pursuit is going to go into places that are multilevel. If you know you can't leap high enough to land on your feet on a loading dock, you're not even going to try. On the other hand, if there is a difference between two planes (like in hilly areas) and you know about it in advance, you can shoot over one and catch many of your pursuers by surprise.

By knowing this stuff about yourself in advance, you're not going to make the mistakes that most people who are stomped make, i.e., try to do a jump, leap, distance, etc., that is beyond your capabilities. The reason most people get caught in hot pursuit is not that they were actually overhauled on the straight stretch, but they did something that slowed them down too much while their pursuers were still going at full speed.

Animal's Law of E & E Number 5: *Don't get fancy*

until you have enough time to make up for the time you're going to lose. Until then it is a straight-out haul ass.

Another real important thing about knowing your limitations is that by doing so, you won't try anything that you can't do. However, the pack behind you won't have done its homework. Just because a guy is strong or a good fighter doesn't mean he's also a track star. In fact, most badasses that I have met have never really bothered to learn how to run correctly. They're out there flailing all over everywhere, while some middle-aged woman who jogs leaves them in the dust. You can weed out a shitload of your pursuers by simply laying out an obstacle course for them, consisting of things that you know you can do.

I know it never happens on TV, but it does get real "three stooges" out there. People run into each other, slip, trip over shit, stumble, knock each other off fences, and (my personal favorite) fall down and trip someone else up. If you know what you can do and avoid things that you can't, you're going to be miles ahead of the competition (namely because they'll be back there falling all over themselves, discovering that they really couldn't clear that fence like they thought they could).

If someone is catching up to you, don't just try to run faster. Obviously the guy is faster, so it's a wasted effort. The "directional change stomp" is familiar to anyone who has ever played tag. This is where you bring your weight down on one leg and bounce off in another direction. Then immediately beeline it to someplace where you can get something to toss behind you. Or, if you can time it right, do a directional stomp in front of a passageway. You suddenly hook a turn down an apartment walkway, and that guy has got to slam on the brakes and then do a turn.

If you want to get flamboyant, and there's only one guy, you can do a drop punch. This works better if the guy is to either side instead of directly behind you. If he's directly behind you, he'll slam into you. If he's to your left, you use your right leg; if he's on your right, use your left. Basically it's where you hook a U-turn and it becomes a punch. Using the leg opposite from the side he's coming up on you, you slam to a stop. Your body weight won't stop you immediately, and if you tried to make it you'd fall on your ass. To handle this energy, you pivot the same side of your body around 180 degrees (right to left/left to right). Your other side spins around behind, and you use that leg as a back brace. While all of this is going on, you're ducking beneath the guy's outstretched arm. As you're dropping into this stance you're sticking your arm out straight. If you can't get that position, a shoulder locked hook also works. In either case you drive one into the guy's bread basket. He's going full steam, so you don't really have to punch; he's going to impale himself on your arm. Most importantly, if you try to punch, you're likely to break your arm and/or wrist. Once you do this move, it's more a case of preparing for impact than punching. Lock up every muscle you

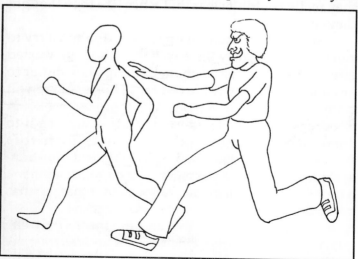

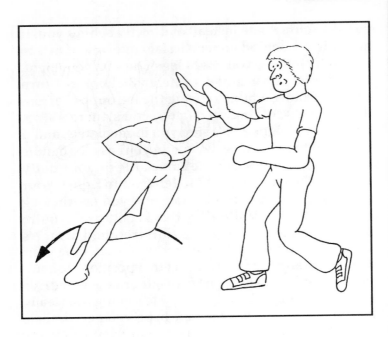

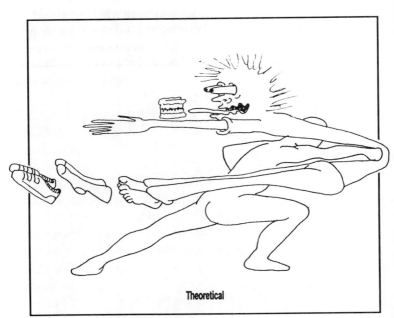

Theoretical

More likely

have in your upper body as he's about to plow into your arm. There comes a release point though. It's where enough energy has been transferred to maul him, but any more and you'll both go over ass over teakettle. At this moment relax and let him fall away from you (help him if he needs it by a shot from your other hand).

This is a flamboyant move, and IT WILL NOT WORK WITHOUT PRACTICE! There are certain speeds past which you will not be able to do it. You have to find out what is your maximum speed to do this without falling over. Another thing that can go wrong is if the guy swerves the wrong way you'll both go bowling over. Finally, the timing has to be perfect. The guy's hand has to be mere inches away from you in order for it to work right. If there's too much room, he'll be able to dodge; too little and you won't be able to execute the move. Without the locking of the limb and some form of chest protection (a catcher's chest

pad works) go out and practice with a friend. Keep
your arm relaxed and merely go for the slap; otherwise, your friend, when he gets his wind back, will
beat you over the head with a baseball bat.

Silly as it may sound, the best way to learn anything I'm going to be talking about in these chapters is
to get some friends and play tag. Yes, I'm talking the
children's game where you dash around the neighborhood. If there are only two of you, take turns; if you
can get a group, everyone chases one person.
Incidentally, if the cops show up, everyone stops,
smiles, and waves. Don't wait for the cop to call you
over; go over to him and tell him what you're doing.
These games look real to the cops, and you have to let
them know that it's just practice.

Notes

1. Unless he's the one who trips over the trash can.

2. While you can read this in a book all you want, it is still better to go out and have someone who is actively doing this maneuver teach you how to do it. Also, gymnastics class is fantastic for surviving all sorts of nasty situations. I highly recommend you go out and have someone show you how to do it first-hand. If nothing else, it's a great way to make friends with badasses).

3. Avoid going over fences without these, as there's no fast or safe way to do it.

4. Incidentally, since you never touched the guy and you didn't hold a gun to his head and force him to chase you, if he gets mauled in the process, tough shit. He doesn't have a legal leg to stand on.

5. The goofy son of a bitch also thinks it's great fun to go run a hundred miles. Sheesh!

CHAPTER FOUR

Bugging Out

"Gimme three steps…"

—The time-honored request
made more famous
by Lynyrd Skynyrd

A
s you may have
noticed by now, the state of the art
with street E&E is to avoid getting
hurt while laying a trail which is
going to get your pursuers hurt if
they try to follow it. You can
achieve this rarefied state by using
the terrain and natural events
around you as much as possible.

Unless you live in Podunkee,
Iowa, one of the most common
items around you is cars (although
Podunkee residents can use cattle
stampedes instead). Let me state
right here that under most circumstances I am against darting out
into the street. It had better be
pretty hairy before you go waltzing out into the four-lane. The reason for this is simple—physics.

You can break the laws of man left, right, up, down and center and suffer no immediate retribution.[1] This makes a whole lot of people arrogant as hell about breaking the law. Let me tell you, children, there is one set of laws you don't even want to try to break, and them's the laws of physics that apply to this plane.

While it may be getting flack on the quantum level, E=MC[2] works well enough in mundane reality; so do the laws of motion.[2] One of the bigger such laws that works just fine dictates that a 3,000-pound car traveling at 40 mph won't be able to stop in 20 feet. I believe the standard equation states that it takes one car length for every 10 miles per hour to effect a complete stop. That means anything inside the required stopping space is going to get hit. According to yet another rule of physics, when car meets human body, the car comes out on top. The human being wedged under the car and cheese-grated on the highway would be a literal translation. As I've mentioned before, the object of E&E is to *escape* damage, not to do it to yourself. Therefore let's look at getting your ass across the street safely while engaged in hot pursuit.

Two perpendicular lines are going to meet at a certain point. Now, for you budding geometricians, using the technical illustration below, I want you to figure

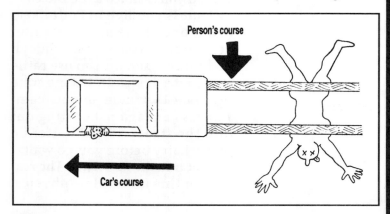

Person's course

Car's course

out the exact point of intersection for the two perpendicular lines (answer on page 430).

As you may have noticed the line of the person's course was interrupted by that of the automobile. This is a clear case for the use of the mathematic symbol of > (greater than). Therefore, the equation is:

car's force > person's force.

Needless to say, it behooves you not to get into such a contest. Crossing the street at a right angle to the flow of traffic is not the best way to keep from becoming a roadside attraction.

The question becomes how to you get across the street without getting smeared. Well, the trick is to use a step pattern. First you parallel the traffic, then you dart across only one lane at a time. Your overall cut across is diagonal rather than perpendicular. Once you reach a divider (whether lane, painted divider, or actual concrete divider), you run along it until another opening comes along for you to utilize. Then you zip across the next lane.

In this way, you parallel the traffic as much as possible. This is better for two reasons: 1) you're less likely to get smashed, and 2) you're less likely to cause an

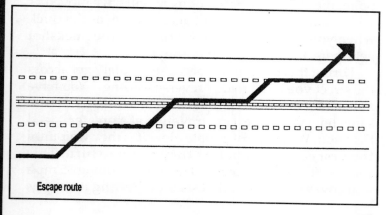

Escape route

accident. If you cause an accident by darting out into the street, you are liable! If the pursuit happens in your neighborhood, you're likely to be recognized. Even though you were being chased, the insurance company will hold you responsible. On the other hand, if one of your pursuers causes an accident or gets run over, that's his problem.

There was a video game called "Frogger," which was a really morbid way to teach people how to get across streets safely. I don't know if it went onto home video or not, but it's a great game to teach this dynamic. If you ever get a chance to play it, I highly recommend it (even though my brother-in-law said I was dating myself by talking about it). The idea is to get a frog across the highway and river so he can get laid. The highway is full of cars, and you have to run parallel to the traffic and cross when it's safe. Like Tetris will teach you how to pack a truck, this game is a great teaching tool, complete with splat marks, squish noises, and skull and crossbones.

If you've ever gone duck hunting, you'll know something already. That is a thing called "leading." Basically, in order to hit a moving object, you have to aim for where it's going to be. By the time your bullet has traveled the distance from you to an intercept point, the object you're shooting at will have moved as well. That's why you don't actually aim at the duck when you pull the trigger. By the time the buckshot gets there, the duck isn't there anymore.

I bring this concept up because to safely get across the street you need to do "reverse leading." You have at least an 8-foot area to cross (car width). On that same line, you have a car traveling at a greater speed than you. Where most people blow it is they wait until the first car is past before they begin to turn. This shaves off at least a second. The next car doing 35 mph will cover 51.3 feet in that second. Putting it simply, unless you want to become a hood ornament, you need that extra second.

Someone once said that the secret to flying is throwing yourself at the earth and missing. Reverse leading is the same thing. You throw yourself at a car and miss. You begin your turn when the car is still in the space you are going to be occupying in a moment. Literally, you aim for its trunk; by the time you get there, it's gone. An important safety tip here: for trucks, shoot for the part of the bed behind the back wheels. That way it's more likely to be gone when you get there.

For thick traffic, not only do I recommend reverse leading but also, believe it or not, hand signals! If you're hauling ass down the lane line, there's a motorist who is probably shitting bricks about your being there. He has no idea what you are about to do. If he panics, he's going to cause a smash-up. While a smash-up might squish a few of your pursuers, a moving line of cars is more effective in keeping them away. (The motorist also might panic and end up squishing you anyway.)

A quick flick of the arm to tell the guy that you're cutting a lane will warn him in advance as to what you're about to do. He's probably already slowing down, and a hand signal is going to let him know that he's on the right course. That will buy you an extra second or two to get across, and remember how much distance a car can cover in a second.

Especially when you are heading *into* oncoming traffic, you should use your hand signals to tell the motorists what you're about to do. To your way of thinking, this chase has been going on for awhile. On the other hand, you've just popped into the motorist's reality. He's is doing 40 miles an hour, and all of a sudden, POOF! You pop out of nowhere, heading straight toward him in a place where you shouldn't be. Again, throwing a quick hand signal lets that person in on what's happening. I should also point out that this includes just going straight down that yellow divider line. If you see a driver coming toward you is getting a little nervous, point forward to tell him you're not going to dart out in front of the car suddenly. (Don't worry about the guys chasing you figuring out what you're doing; they've probably guessed by now anyway.)

Truth of the matter is, you're going to interrupt traffic by jumping out into it. If, however, you *stop* the traffic, you have taken all the risks and left your pursuers a walk in the park to come after you. Where's the motivation to let you go in that? No, no, no,—if they're going to chase you into the street, they get to play tag with moving cars too. If they don't know about things like reverse leading and lane stepping, let them find out the hard way. There is a distinct *"screeech . . . thud!"* associated with a body hitting the hood that will attract the attention of even the most committed pursuers. People slow down and stare at accidents involving complete strangers; you can bet that one of their friends getting plastered on the hood of a car is an event that is going to catch their attention. Animal's Law of E&E Number 6: *Always parallel traffic before you jump into it.*

Don't worry about the guys behind you making it across the street at the same time as you do. If you're ahead of them, the cars that affect you are different than the ones they have to deal with. By paralleling the traffic, you've been able to choose the best moment for you to cross, not them.

While we're on the subject of automobiles, let's chat about how to ditch them. Cars are interesting things to get away from. Most people realize a very important fact too late: cars can move faster than we can. That's the bad news. The good news is that they are actually limited in how they can move.

Perhaps the best way to explain this would be to look at a chessboard—the bishop, to be specific. Now the bishop can move an unlimited number of squares along the same line of colored squares it's on. If you are on the same line, you can be creamed from all the way across the board. However, if you aren't on a same-color square, the bishop can't touch you. You can be standing on the square right next to it and be safe. Pfffftt!!!

How does this relate to evading a car? A street is one of those lines that a car can travel on. It does so at a much higher rate of speed than you can. The art of getting away from a car is in moving where it can't go. If it's running up and down, you move side to side.

The way to get away from a car is to cut across the spaces between the streets. This is one of the few times in E&E when you use a right angle to get away from your pursuer. If a car shows up with a group looking for you, you don't run along the street! You peel off at a 90-degree angle immediately. This is where most people blow it. Instead of immediately cutting across, they boogie down the street. This allows the car to catch up to them and the folks inside to pile out and give foot chase.

The car's higher speed eats up most of the head start the person could have had. The victim realizes too late that he should have cut across instead of running down the street.

In suburban areas, this means you go tripping through people's yards, front and back. You jump a few fences, and you're the next street over. In urban areas you flash through some apartment buildings/complexes and, believe it or not, even some businesses. Now, another important safety tip: once you've cleared out of a street and landed on the next one, keep going in the same direction (perpendicular to the street). Don't stop at just one street; clear two or three before you begin to travel in the same direction as the streets again. Even if people jump out and give chase, the car is going to circle the block. It's going to do this rather quickly. If you stop after the first street, that car is going to catch up to you. However, if you've put a few streets between you and your pursuers, they're going to spend time cruising the other streets looking for you.

If everyone stays in the car (which, if you've gotten out of there soon enough, will be the case), they will cruise for you! If you put enough of a lead on them, they're going to stay in the car rather than jump out and chase you. If they think they know where you're going, they're more likely to make this lazy mistake. Problem is, when they show up you're not there.

Animal's Law of E&E Number 7: *Never, ever try to outrun a car on its own terms!* If a car catches you in a parking lot, keep out of the lanes, and cut across diagonally so it will eat itself on the cement tire stops. Make a car go over curbs and drops and it'll eat its suspension. (In case you didn't know, if a streetcar leaves the ground by more than 6 inches its suspension is blown to hell.) In parking lots don't be afraid to double back on your trail to keep them dealing with the concrete stops. Often people who do this are either stoned or have been drinking. The longer they're in an area, the more likely they are to screw up and sacrifice their undercarriage to the tire stop god.

Now let's look at something important. If you bolt from a car in a business district, you're probably going to have to go through a shop. Most states require businesses to have two exits. This has to do with fires and people getting trapped in burning buildings. While this may be the law, the truth of the matter may be a little different. It is extremely likely that the back way will be locked and/or alarmed. More often than not, though, it'll be through a storage area. This might slow you down a bit. Also, for politeness' sake, you should broadcast your intentions and destination to the shopkeeper. People are prone to get upset if you dash through their place of business without good reason. Yelling for them to call 911 will usually get them off your back.

It also serves to give them some measure of protection and time to prepare if the fan club follows you. I once knew a guy who got blown away when a running gang fight came down the street. A kid ducked into the liquor store where the guy worked to reload his gun. The guy said, "Hey, you can't come in here," and the gangster shot him. It was too bad; he was a nice guy. Take a hint: you don't tell someone in the middle of a firefight what he can and can't do. If you've alerted people that something is wrong, they're less likely to do something stupid like that.

Generally back doors of businesses will drop you into either a parking lot or an alley, sometimes both. Do not linger in an area where a car can reach you. Generally, the back of a business will abut either another business or a residential area. In either case, you will likely be facing at least an 8-foot obstacle. It is common for residents to either build walls or solid fences to screen their view of neighboring businesses. Do not hesitate to use any available car, trash can, or pallet collection to aid you in getting over this obstacle. It is critical to get out of there as fast as you can, as there's undoubtedly a way for a car to access the area.

Another thing to consider is that you are more likely to encounter barbed wire in business districts than you are in the suburbs. You might have just rabbited into an enclosed area that will tear you up if you try to go over. In which case, you're going to have to double back and try to get out the front way. Now the good news is, unless you've been playing with the *really* bad boys, they won't pursue you into a business. Most people, if they see you do a full-tilt boogie into a business, are probably going to circle around rather than follow you in.[3] Again, when you find yourself on the street, do not parallel it. Cross the street and do the exact thing you were going to do originally, but in the other direction! If they don't see you in the alley, they're going to come looking again on the street. By that time, you should be a few blocks over.

Now another thing which you might want to try, especially in suburban areas, is to hook a U-turn. Everybody in the car sees you bolt into someone's backyard. What they don't see is, instead of hitting the back fence and heading to the next street over, you hit the side fence and hop into the next yard. You do this at least twice (unless you suffer canine interruptus) to prevent your accidentally encountering anyone who's pursuing on foot. Then you bolt back across the street you just came from and buy some space in the other direction. Make sure the coast is clear and the car has gone in search of you along your original course before you pop back onto the street. Your fan club will have hours of fun looking for you in an entirely different direction than where you are.

Let's take another look at what most people do to get caught when they're being pursued. After slowing down to go over obstacles at the wrong time, the next biggest reason people get caught during pursuits is they turn on right angles. Animal's Law of E&E Number 8: *The only time you do a right-angle turn is when triangulation is impossible.* Let us, for a moment, look at the illustration on the facing page.

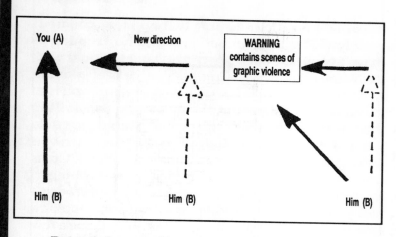

Point A (pursued) and point B (pursuer) are going along on the same course. In the second one, A decides to hook a left. Now here's the 64,000-dollar question: what does B have to do in order to land on A's ass? THAT'S RIGHT! THE ANSWER IS TRIANGULATE! As shown in frame three, B only has to travel down the third side of the triangle to nail little old A's ass to the wall! Isn't that exciting?!

Most people seriously blow it on this one. In an open area they try for the 90-degree turn, forgetting that the pursuers only have to alter their course to converge at the same point. Any lead that you might have had you just kissed off by hookin' a 90. The only time it's safe to make a 90-degree turn is when the homeboys also have to do it. This is only accomplished by seriously big obstructions like buildings and cliffs. Look at the illustrations on the next page for an example.

In the first one, the building prevented Mr. B from triangulating. In the second one, however, the car wasn't big enough to keep it from happening. In the second one, the only thing that A accomplished by using the car in this situation is to screw himself by thinking it would stop B.

In hot pursuit there are only diagonals. If you come

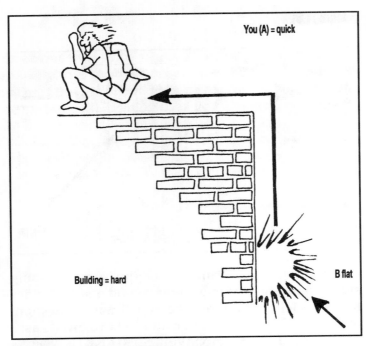

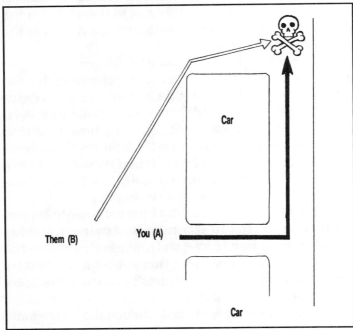

to a corner, you cut it. If you're bulleting across an empty street, you shoot diagonally from corner to corner. If you are going to dart between cars, you come at them from an angle. You keep going in the same direction afterward, too.

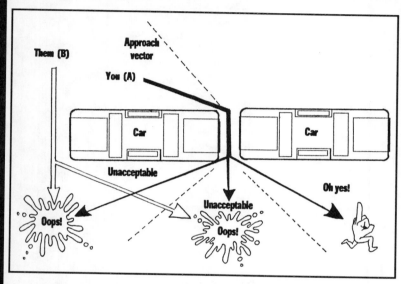

Look at the illustration and try to figure out how the Bs could triangulate on A. The answer is, they can't. Not only can't they cut him off at the pass, but they are going to bottleneck getting through the gap between cars. If, however, A did a very silly thing and shot off perpendicular to the line of cars, then he'd be able to be triangulated on.

When you walk through an area, look at it from the standpoint of diagonals rather than right angles. You're supposed to walk parallel to the street and cross at the corners (lines and angles); this affects how we view our terrain. Now look at it from the perspective of diagonal lines to get through it in the quickest way possible. You can cut through a neighborhood in half the time using diagonals as opposed to 90-degree angles. To tell you the truth, it isn't because most people are slow runners that they get caught; it's because they are sloppy about triangulation. They're running a longer course than the guys behind them; no wonder they get caught.

Notes

1. Not because, as many criminals think, the cops are stupid, but because they are too busy with the serious bad guys to concentrate on the minor players. Occasionally, the cops get a chance to focus on the small fry, and when they do they usually go through them like shit through a goose. It's easy to get away with shit when people are too busy to come after you. Don't mistake that for talent.

2. Even though the first one is unprovable in physical reality. Want to have fun at parties? Mention that to a scientist: "You can't prove your first law, neener, neener, neener!"

3. If they do follow you, you're back to the phase 1-type of evasion, that of surviving the nose-to-nose encounter. The normal maxim still generally works: "Head for the lights and people to shake pursuers."

CHAPTER FIVE

Thinnin' the Herd

"What causes opponents to come of their own accord is the prospect of gain. What discourages opponents from coming is the prospect of harm."

—Sun Tzu
The Art of War

Up to this point I've been talking generalities that apply to one or many pursuers. It's now time to look at shaking a few of these chumps off your tail. You may be able to fight one (possibly two), but you aren't going to be able to handle four or five. Therefore, you're going to have to do something to thin the herd.

One guy catching up to you while five guys are strung out behind you isn't as big a problem as all six grabbing you at once. Even if the point guy is a faster runner than you are, it only takes one trash can to fuck up his day real bad. On the other hand, if six pounce on you at once, one trash can isn't going to be enough. It is in your best interest to get these guys thinned down as fast as possible.

While inherent running ability (or the lack of it) is going to do wonders for thinnin' the herd over a distance, you can really help the process along. The number-one, primo tool for the job is a thing called a bottleneck. Simply put, five guys cannot simultaneously pass through a gap only wide enough for one person! Either they are going to have to slow down and file through or find an alternative route. In either case, you'd be amazed at the three-stooges quality of the process. I've seen people slam into each other, slip, trip, and nosedive when they get bottlenecked.

As any general of any age can tell you, it's slower to move more people than it is just one. In that fact lies your main advantage, especially around bottlenecks. A bottleneck can occur between cars, shrubs, buildings, gates, doorways, bridges, or anything else you can think up. Anywhere only a single person can pass at a time can be used to slow your pursuers down.

Go ahead and shoot the gap as much as you can. Once you do that, you're going to start stringing them out and thinnin' them. If you shoot the gap between two shrubs in a hedge, the odds are at least one of the guys is going to try to shoot another gap that isn't wide enough. Boom, one guy is hung up in the bushes. If you're lucky, a would-be Jim Thorpe is going to try to hurdle it and discover why you tuck your back leg up when you jump stuff. (A trailing back leg will snag up and slam you face-down faster than superglue.) This is how you thin the herd by using bottlenecks.

Also, bottlenecks are the happenin' place to leave obstacles. A dragged-over shopping cart left behind you in a parking lot isn't much of a problem to anyone who isn't immediately behind you. On the other hand, that same shopping cart in a narrow alley is a hassle for everyone behind you. There is nothing like shooting through an open gate and slamming it shut behind you for slowing folks down. The same thing can be said for dragging doors shut behind you. Furniture is also loads of fun to leave behind you. Nothing like tripping over a chair to take the wind out of someone's sails.[1] Incidentally, for real nasty situations, people also work as obstacles in your pursuers' paths. Since it's likely to get the person who is used hurt, I advise you to use someone you don't like rather than an innocent.

(Free tip here: with hedges it's usually better to leap and turn your hips sideways. The branches are thicker down near the bottom where your feet would be if you didn't jump. Thick branches can trip you real easily. The reason you trip is your body weight is still moving forward while your feet are staying still. Pick the feet up and this problem goes away. Your entire body clears any resistance all at once. Turning sideways allows the more narrow part of your body to shoot the gap [that is, unless you really dig Oreo cookies]. The thinner the object going through a gap, the less likely it is to get hung up. Finally, your jacket is more likely to cling to your body if you're going sideways. If you're shooting through straight, your jacket will be streaming out behind you near your waist. That means it's more likely to get snagged up! The twisting action you did to get your body sideways will usually tighten up your jacket and remove this problem. The same thing goes with baggy pants. Come to think of it, let's talk about your threads for a second. If you are wearing baggy things, *don't try to shoot snaggy gaps!* Cars are usually fine if they don't have stuff on their front ends; however, pointy fences and prickly hedges should be avoided if possible. If you gotta wiggle under a fence, take your jacket off before you hit the hole. Snags do happen a lot during pursuit. The best you can hope for

STREET E & E

is to rip the shit out of your clothes, but the worst is when they catch you because you're hung up. If it comes to this, do a lizard and leave that jacket there.)[2]

Stairs are the next thing that is of critical importance. If you approach them the right way, you can shake out a few pursuers. Generally, I say avoid dashing up or down stairs in pursuits. However, sometimes ya gotta do what ya gotta do. The main reason for avoiding them is, of course, reduced speed. You're slowing down while your pursuers are still coming at you full-speed-ahead. However, there exists another problem. Most people fuck up on stairs by not paying attention to what they are doing! This is why folks trip on stairs, especially at high speeds. I want you to try something. Stand up and walk across the room. Now, instead of simply telling your body, "Walk," take manual control of the process. Consciously shift balance, lift leg, counterbalance, extend leg, shift foot for impact, shift balance forward to create step, repeat. Harder to do, isn't it?

If you were to try that move on stairs, you'd probably kill yourself. Yet everyday we subconsciously walk up stairs without batting an eye. Our body knows what to do, and we let it run things without paying attention. It is an unconscious process and, under normal circumstances, quite adequate. Unfortunately, during hot pursuit that same assumption is a disaster waiting to happen. Without thinking about it, people hit the stairs at high speed and have their attention elsewhere. If you're driving your car slowly, it's no big thing if your mind is somewhere else, but if you're doing 110, you had better be paying attention to what you're doing! The same thing applies to walking up stairs and running up them.

You may have 20 people on your ass, but when you hit those stairs, the only thing you're thinking of is those stairs! At that moment, everything else falls

104

away just for a second and your eyes are glued on that next step! This is concentration on only one thing! The reason people eat it on stairs is they are going over rough terrain and they are looking elsewhere instead of where their feet are going. It's not the top of the stairs you need to be watching, but the next step your foot is going to land on! If you're screaming along worrying more about the guys behind you than getting over those stairs, you're setting yourself up to trip! The second you clear those stairs, you widen your perspective out again and haul ass out of there, but until then, keep it focused!

Like I said, if you do this right, you can lose a few of the herd. Some of those that don't trip will slow down as they shift their perspective to getting up the stairs. There will probably be one or two jokers who have sufficient physical coordination to get up the stairs without slowing, but this will thin them out a bit.

A similar opportunity exists with terrain. It is faster to run over concrete than it is over iceplant. In the same vein, it is faster to run over hard ground than sand. The terrain you go through will affect your speed. Running along a dirt path, you will be moving faster than your pursuers, who are either single file on the path behind you or crashing through the weeds. You can run straight on ice, but the turns are going to be a bitch.[3] The terrain you're cutting through will affect your speed.

The same rule that governs going over obstructions and jumping also applies to shifting terrain: don't do it unless you have sufficient lead to compensate for your reduced speed while your pursuers are still going at full tilt. Stairs, sand, ground foliage, inclines, ice, snow, and water will all affect your speed (and theirs, but not till you've had your turn). If they're too close, they'll catch you.

Whenever you go into supernasty terrain, you have

to have the same mind-set as when you're going up and down stairs; that is, focus on where your feet are going. I once got chased over some rocks at the Marina Del Rey jetties ("Toes Beach," so named because the jetties look like toes). I was squirreling over the rocks, intent on only my hand and feet placement, while the guys behind me were tearing their asses up. They were trying to watch me instead of where they were going. That pursuit only lasted about a hundred linear feet before I was out of danger. They got banged up for their troubles.

The first cousin of terrain is the obstacle course. In a park there are trees, trash cans, picnic tables, young lovers wrestling on the grass, and so on, that can be used to your advantage. While it's hard to get someone to run into a tree in broad daylight, at night one of those above-ground water mains makes for a nasty surprise. The trick for an obstacle course is to make your pursuers weave and bob as much as possible to avoid bottlenecks while you're heading in as straight a line as possible. Make them spread wide behind you, then turn it against them. Shave close to things to string them out. Let's say there are four guys spread out behind you and you shave past a picnic table to your left. The guys on your eight o'clock will either have to slow down to fall behind the guys to the right or take extra steps to the left to get around the table. Going over it also slows them down and increases their chances for sprained ankles.

Wander around and look at things that you could turn to your advantage in a pursuit. Look at it from the standpoint of how three guys would have to get through an area instead of just one. While I was writing this book I wandered around my neighborhood for three hours systematizing the core rules of E & E. My neighbors thought I was nuts standing in front of a line of cars for 20 minutes figuring out approach vectors. I'm real expressive with my hands, so I was standing in the street waving my arms, directing imaginary pursuits. I'm amazed they didn't call the cops.

Let's take a walk over to the Biology Department for a moment and look at our friend the cheetah. You will notice that Mr. Four on the Floor is the fastest land animal on this planet. You will also notice in fact that Speed Racer here is, for the big cat department, really rather small. In fact, cheetahs' jaws aren't really strong enough to effectively kill the size antelope they prey on. If that's the case, how do homey do it?

The answer is simple. Cheetahs kill by tripping their prey. An antelope doing a nosedive at 45 mph is generally a dead antelope. Fortunately, most human pursuers prefer grabbing you and dragging you down over tripping you. (If this tripping biz gets out to the wolf packs, it could spell trouble for the home team. But evidently it isn't as fun watching someone maul themselves as a result of your tripping them as it is to beat them to a bloody pulp by hand, so I wouldn't worry about that happening soon.)

Just because the Bozo Brigade doesn't use tripping techniques, however, doesn't mean you shouldn't take a hint from Mr. Cheetah. A trash can or shopping cart thrown or dragged over into someone's legs means laughing boy is going to be eating his teeth. You have to be a real asshole to run past one of your buds who's just skidded 10 feet on his face.

If you wing a two-by-four into someone's legs at top speed, it's hospital time for the little buckaroo. Most of his buddies are going to slow down to check that action out. Not only because one of their own got hurt, but because their prey just grew teeth. I've said before and I'll say it again—it's a different game when the other side shoots back. Most people aren't going to risk it when they think they're going to get hurt if they keep it up.

One important point: until that mob you're running from has strung out a little bit, you don't want to do anything that will slow you down. Animal's Law of E&E Number 9: *If you have more than three pursuers within a hundred feet, don't go for anything lower than a waist-level grab.* A trash can you can just drag over as you shoot past. All you do is snake your arm out and toss it over. The same thing with a shopping cart. If someone is closing on you, you drop it directly into his path. Don't bother to turn around to watch him fly, either; just keep going. Slamming gates behind you is also loads of laughs. Certain kinds will lock, and your pursuers have to reach over and grope around to find the latch.

Don't forget to look up, either. Dragging stuff off the top shelf at the supermarket is definitely effective. Ever tried to run through an obstacle course of cans and broken glass with pickle juice on your shoes? If the opportunity magically presents itself, dragging a shelf down on someone is worth a million laughs.[4] While it's more fun to drop things on people's heads while they are chasing you for nefarious purposes, just leaving a whirling trail of chaos behind you does tend to slow them down. (Also, if you drag something down onto someone at the beginning of the chase, it's not clear to witnesses that you were in danger. However, if everyone sees you being chased and someone accidently trips over a trash can or slips in pickle juice he stepped in while chasing you, that's his tough luck.)

The waist-level grab allows you to leave litter behind you while not reducing your escape speed. If there are more than three people behind you, you don't want to lose any time. If you have the numbers down to one or two inside a hundred feet, then you can begin to go for stuff at lower levels.

The gauchos of Bolivia have a nasty object called the bolo. It was adopted from the Indian tribes, who originally used it for hunting. Three long straps with weights attached to them make for a nasty flying surprise. While it can crush a man's skull, the normal target is a horse's or cow's legs. The bolo basically comes like a whirling helicopter blade into the legs of the target. Something traveling in a horizontal rotary path is pure hell to avoid. Chains, sticks, branches, two-by-fours, boards, etc., all rotor real nicely. If you've thinned the herd enough through natural terrain that you're down to one or two main pursuers, it's time to turn the tables. If you rotor blade objects into someone's legs while he's at a dead run, you'll bring him down like a ton of bricks.

It is when you get into lower-level objects that the shit is going to get seriously ugly. It is at this time that the flight aspect has suddenly turned to the fight aspect. While they are still hunting, so are you. It's now a game of hit and run. You're now hunting the guy in front. I gotta tell you, this is the time that people get killed in this business. Someone can eat a trash can at high speed and just get a hospital trip out of it. He might die, but tough shit. On the other hand, if you're waiting around a corner with a two-by-four, the odds are that he's going down permanently. Braining him at a full run makes it almost a certainty.

I'm serious about it not turning into a stand-up fight yet. You only stay there long enough to nail one guy before you're winging off again. Even if there are two guys neck-and-neck, if you take out one, the other guy will, 99 times out of a 100, geek. Even if he's the baddest dude there, he's got a choice: help his partner or chase you. All but the most psychotic will choose the former. And if Chuckles keeps it up, he's next. The next corner he comes around may have his name on it, and there are very few people who are so psychotic that this won't slow them down.

The odds are that the rest of the group coming

around the corner will see Bonzo standing there staring at the wet spot and stop as well. Most of the time,
if you hurt one of theirs badly, the pursuit will stop for
the moment. You'll have signed yourself up for a long-
standing war, but this round is over.

Speaking of which, let's look at something I just
said. There are three basic ways that this kind of war
will end (I'm talking game over, finito, over, done): 1)
They get you. You're dead and that's that. 2) You move
out of the area This means you both physically relo-
cate to where these people are not and you no longer
run in the same circles. You're in different places; you
can't fight. Physical impossibility. 3) You hurt them so
badly that they back off. If you find your ass in this
crack and you can't get the hell out of dodge, you
gotta go to war. You can't expect these people to merely forgive and forget that you mauled one of theirs
while they were chasing you. If you do, you'll have a
target on your chest until option number 1 is achieved.

(The truth of the matter is, the war I had with the
Venice surfers ended with a combination of number 2
and number 3, with 2 being the main reason the game
came to a close. First school finished, and we all grad-
uated. That meant we no longer had to meet on common ground. They stayed near Venice Beach, and I cut
out to Hollywood. The last time one of them got a
piece of me was six months after school let out. I had
been kicking at a shopping mall, and I got nailed from
behind by a guy who flew off before I could get back
up. That's why the final score was 2 to 1—the fuckers
finally got a piece out of me.)

I personally recommend option two. Warfare is
mostly a matter of convenience. Unless you've really
screwed the pooch, the odds are that the bad boys
aren't going to leave their home turf to come looking
for you: A) it's too much work, and B) they might get
their asses shot for coming into someone else's hood.

(Actually, B is much more real than many people think it is, and it affects how they operate.) I can tell you from personal experience that you don't want to try either of the other two options. The first one seriously cuts down on your chances of getting laid, while the last turns you into something seriously warped. The reason I get along with Vietnam vets is we both know what it's like being hunted in a guerrilla-warfare setting. You gotta be committed to taking your enemies down, and that marks you for life.

(Incidentally, I'd like to do a public service announcement for kids who have found themselves in the same situation as I did. Take this book to your folks and let them read it, especially this paragraph. When the shit went down for me, I went to both my mom and my real dad and asked for help. My mom was too busy trying to keep our heads above water to pay it much mind, and my dad thought I was exaggerating the threat. They came up with the lame-assed answer of, "We'll take it to the principal if you want." Yeah, right! I bet that'll have those guys shaking in their boots. Basically, I was stuck getting my ass out of the situation. My answer to all of this was that by the time I left Venice at the ripe old age of 20, I had buried three friends, been shot at twice, been through three knife fights, stabbed one guy, clubbed two more into the hospital, and bare-handed hospitalized two others. *That's how fucking serious it was!* To tell you the truth, I wasn't that much of a badass, either; I was considerably more mellow than many. That was when I was younger, and I can tell you it's gotten a shitload worse out there. Go to the library and look up the Uniform Crime Report and see how many murders are committed by people under 21. The world is getting really gonzo out there, and there are teen sociopaths who consider killing someone a mark of manhood. If your kid is coming to you asking for help, look into it without the blinders of adulthood. It may be a whole lot easier to get him/her the hell out of the neighborhood. I can tell you, this sort of thing stays with you for the rest of your life. Public service announcement over.)

The way to take out a pursuer in this sort of situation is through a blind.[5] While a rotoring two-by-four can be done anywhere, I still recommend you pick it up and scurry around a blind corner. Someone coming around a corner has fewer options as to where he can go and less time to make the decision. If, however, he sees you winding up, he's going to know something is wrong and begin to coast aside. He comes around the corner and you're down a ways, wound up, and waiting, he's got a serious problem, no? The advantage to that is, once you wing it at him you can still beat feet and you have a safety distance to boot. This sort of thing is really useful if there are two of them running neck and neck.

Any view cut can be used to set up a trap. Even if you're going to turn and nail the SOB, see what you can do about picking up something before the trap. That way all you have to do is choose the location, rather than casting around for a weapon and choosing the best strike point. Remember, your pursuit is going to be getting there uncomfortably fast. If you're not ready for them, all you've done is allowed yourself to get caught.

That's why it is better to do only one thing at a time. If you scoop up a weapon, that's going to take up time—time you can afford, but still time spent. When you run again, that buys you back some time. Now you're back to running even. That will give you more time to choose the best spot to counterattack from. Needless to say, you're only going to get one shot at it, so you had better make it count.

If you have a long club, a baseball swing is acceptable. However, a bottle, pot, or rock should be used in a downward strike (diagonal ones seem to work best, as they are harder to dodge). If the person has a weapon, start your strike before he clears the corner. If you wait until he can see you, he might be able to bring his weapon to bear and get off a shot. Again, I have to warn you that cranial impact can easily lead to death, so 1) before you do it, make sure that you're justified, and 2) make sure there are no witnesses. If someone sees you do it, you've got a murder rap on your hands.

Now I got some good news and I got some bad news. The good news is, if the guys after you are hardcore, established, and organized gang types, they aren't going to squeal on you. They'd prefer to do you personally. The bad news is if it's just a pack of low-life scum that hang together, if you off one of them they're going to squeal like pigs. It's the fuckin' amateurs who are shocked when they discover that this game works both ways. They'll happily put you in a hospital for three months, but when you brain one of their buddies they go running to the police. Often when they're standing there with their thumbs up their asses, staring at their buddy's body in total shock, a cop will walk up and say, "Your ass is in trouble, now who did this?" At which point, Poindexter will blurt out your name. At this point, it isn't likely that street justice will apply; you're going to court.

If someone dies while chasing you because they "tripped," you're less likely to get in trouble than if people saw you crack the guy over the gourd.[6] This is why it is usually better to rotor something into their legs rather than bash 'em inna head. Even if you get dragged into court, you can plead self-defense and/or involuntary manslaughter rather than murder.

Notes

1. What, you don't think pursuits happen indoors? Ha! Have you got a thing or two to learn. Why do you think the Samurai wore both long and short swords? The short were for fighting indoors.

2. Some lizards have detachable tails, which they drop when something grabs onto them. This safety release often saves their lives.

3. This is another reason diagonals are better than right-angled turns, you're less likely to end up on your ass in snow and ice.

4. Unfortunately, a lawsuit as well. That's why you always "saw" a knife in his hand when you make a formal statement. You were in fear for your life, *capisce*?

5. Also, if you're in a blind spot there are no witnesses. A good lawyer in court can make that work for you: "Did you actually see my client swing the two-by-four?" "No." "Then how do you know your buddy didn't just trip?" Even if your victim lives, it's his word against yours.

6. You'd be amazed how many times the fact that you dragged the trash can over gets left off the report. That's what they call it—street justice.

CHAPTER SIX

Disappearing

"Man, you ninjaed! I was behind you, watching, then zip! Next second, I'm standing there going, 'Where'd he go?"

—Chris Colin, my backup, after seeing me disappear to reach an objective

One of my specialties is to disappear from sight. I can evaporate faster than a politician's promise. I once crashed at my bro Tim's house and disappeared in plain sight.

Both he and his wife searched the entire house but couldn't find where I was sleeping. I was sacked out in the front room near the couch. When I finally decided I couldn't sleep anymore with them crashing around, I got out of the bedding and went to cage a cup of coffee. Tim's first words to me were, "Where the fuck were you?" I pointed to the pile of blankets in plain sight and said, "There." He was shocked that he hadn't been able to find me.

Disappearing is a talent that the hunted must have; however, it is also a talent that successful hunters must have. The best hunters are those who can slip up and snake out of nowhere to nail their prey. It's the hunter who comes out of nowhere and doesn't give you a chance who is the most dangerous. The swaggering loudmouth you see coming from a mile away is more of a pain in the ass than a danger. Ninja were the best at this example of the silent hunter. Once you learn how to disappear as the hunted, then you need to work on disappearing as the hunter.[1]

There are several tricks to disappearing, and most of them have to do with how someone else perceives things. The stage magician specializes in distracting your attention to one part while doing something else over there. Everyone knows this and accepts it as how a magician operates. With only a slight tweak of that rule, we can learn how to disappear in the street.

The real trick to disappearing is simple, in fact it's a law. Animal's Law of E & E Number 10: *The best way to hide is along the lines of what someone expects to see.* If somebody expects to see something, they'll accept it without question; however, if they don't see what they expected, or something is amiss with it, they're going to get curious. In disappearing, you don't want someone to get curious.

The difference between disappearing during pursuit and disappearing when you sneak up on someone has to do with that person's expectations. A sentry who is standing on guard expects to see certain stationary bumps on the landscape. If he sees an extra bump or a moving bump, he's going to suspect something is not right with that picture.[2]

What about the guy who's chasing you, though? What does he expect to see? Your butt shaking it down the highway is what he's expecting to see. Failing that, however, he's going to look for your passage! He's going to become a tracker and try to figure out which way you went. To get away, you need to leave a false trail!

People, when they pass through an area, disturb it. A 170-pound body is going to rattle some stuff as it passes. It is this disturbance down one of the possible ways that you went that your pursuers are going to be looking for. Once they see it, they will continue the hunt down that path.

Let's look at a simple example of a crowd. Someone blazing through a crowd will leave a wake of confused and shocked people. As you run through a crowd, even if you don't knock people over, you're going to interrupt a few people's paths and attract attention. This interrupts the normal flow of the crowd. The guys following you are going to be looking for this interruption. While the rest of the crowd is moving normally, people standing there looking in the direction you went blaze your trail. Even if your pursuers lose sight of you momentarily, this is one of the main things they are going to look for. It's called "proof of passage."

Often in pursuit, your pursuers will lose sight of you for a space of a few moments. When this happens they are going to expect to see or hear some sign of which way you went (proof of passage). If not a disturbance, at least a route that you might have taken to explain them still not seeing you. If they don't see this, they know something is wrong, and they will quit running and start looking.

This is why hiding in a dead-end alley is not a good idea. Someone is going to look at the possibilities and say, "Something is wrong. There's no way he could have gotten out of here." They're going to figure out that you're hiding somewhere in the alley. That means he and his buddies are going to start tearing it apart. I can tell you that anyplace you've decided on and gotten into in less than three seconds is not going to bear close scrutiny.

Hollywood has done wonders for screwing up our ideas about ditching pursuit by hiding. I'll give you a sterling example. A lot of people blow it when they come to a three-way intersection. Instead of trucking down a route, they do what someone does in the movies and try to hide. If these guys suddenly pull up and ask, "Which way did he go," they are standing on your hiding spot! Animal's Law of E&E Number 11: *Don't let them lose incentive near your hiding spot!* It's likely that somebody will kick a trash can over in anger, and there you are, "Uh . . . hi guys!"[3]

A two-second hiding space works only if your pursuers flash by your hiding space! You need to do something to lead them away from where you are hiding. This is why the swinging apartment gate worked for the guys after me. They had seen me go one way, heard the gate slam open, and when they got there they saw what they thought was sign of passage. With that they continued on, thinking that they were still pursuing me.

Now I have to tell you, luck was with me on that one. It led into a snakey-lane condominium complex where they could have easily lost sight of me. While they were running through it, I was booking back the other way. By the time they realized they had lost me, they had traveled way beyond where I had actually ditched them. However, sometimes a false trail like that will only buy you a few seconds. If they run into an empty box courtyard and you're not in it, they're going to figure out that you pulled a sneaky. If the front figures out what happened before the tail passes you, you're screwed. Again, they all stop and hang out on top of your hiding place.

Noise, open gates, freshly dumped trash cans, things knocked over, swinging doors, and open windows, etc., are all indicators that someone recently passed that way in a great hurry. If you can create some of these down the direction that you want someone to go, you will do wonders for the effectiveness of your hiding space. Your pursuers will see it and flash right by you.

Another reason people will stop to search is that it takes time to cover certain distances. If everyone sees you dart down a way that leads to a wide-open space, they are going to expect to see you legging it across the said space when they round the corner. If they come busting out and see a wide space of nothing, that does indicate that maybe you didn't go across the area like they were supposed to believe (in which case they're going to start searching for you near where they last saw you).

Animal's Law of E & E Number 12: *Don't try to hide in an area you would not have had time to get out of in the time it took for your pursuers to come into view!* If there is anything that fucks people up in hiding it is this! I'll tell you, a Dumpster is a great place to hide, but if it's in a long blind alley with no exits, they're going to figure out something ain't right. If they've only lost sight of you for two seconds and it's a seven-second run to clear the alley, it's sort of obvious where you are.

Depending on the situation (or how stupid they are), you may want to rabbit out of a hiding spot immediately or dig in even further. If you opt for the boogie, do as many view-cut moves as possible between where you were and where you're going. It'll do you no good if you do a quick ditch and when they back up they see you running down the street. When they come back to where they last saw you, don't still be visible from that place.

I'll tell you, the real problem with hiding is that you suddenly lose control over whether you're found or not. It depends on what they do. If they get pissed and tear up the area (and they often do because of adrenaline—watch *Lethal Weapon* 2), and you're still there hiding, you may get caught. On the other hand, they may thunder out of there immediately trying to find you. In one scenario, if you've dug in, it goes bad for you. In another, if you've immediately rabbited out, it goes bad. Sometimes what you choose works; sometimes it doesn't. Again, there are no guarantees in this business.

What you *can* do, however, is be one rude-assed surprise if they find you. It's the same as stepping on a rattlesnake. When they find you you, zap whoever found you and boogie. That'll turn it to a number 1-type pursuit (where they have a member down[4]). Often this is a problem, however, as many hiding spaces aren't easy to get out of as quickly as they are to get in. You can jump into a Dumpster real fast; getting out, however, is a bit slower. The good news is that in Dumpsters you can find all sorts of neat things to hit people with. If you come out swinging low at their knees, you're more likely to hit, and it's harder to chase someone with a bashed knee than a bashed arm.

Another point about hiding, while it may sound woo-woo, has a solid biological basis: *don't look at your pursuers!* The actual reason has to do with how our brains work. Deep in our think tanks, we have a thing called a cerebral cortex, a.k.a. monkey brain. When we were little more than rodents, someone made an evolutionary decision. That is, land predators will have their eyes in the front, and herbivores will have eyes on the side of their heads. That means predators will look out of the bushes with two eyes. *Our monkey brains still recognize that threat!* This is why the eyes are the hardest thing to camouflage. We instinctively look for eye patterns, and that pattern is easiest for us to spot!

Now I'm sort of in a quandary here. There are two ways of looking at what I'm about to say here. One is almost quantum physics but sounds more scientific, and the other is woo-woo. Another reason you don't want to look at your pursuers while hiding is they can sense you! The scientific explanation for this is that our nervous system is actually an electrochemical network. With this system we create something which can be called electroradiation. We human beings do have energy fields. While empirical scientists are convinced we can't sense this field, quantum physicists aren't so sure (neither are psychics or anyone who has been through the shit). If your electrochemical radiation field impacts someone else's, it is possible someone will sense it. If you've ever felt that someone was looking at you, and turned to see him doing so, you have an idea of what I'm talking about.

The woo-woo explanation is that your pursuers sense your chi focused on them. This is a more succinct way of putting it, but it does turn many people off. A more down-home way of saying it is, "Don' lookit 'em boy, they might get a feelin!'" I've said it before, people on the street are superstitious—they believe in the psychic and magic. After some form of superconsciousness has saved your life, you end up believing in it too.

While getting them to admit it is like pulling teeth, the pros use this stuff all the time. There's a coded language that people use to talk about it. Most people won't admit to it openly, but even down in the most Fundamentalist Bible Belt South you'll find folks who have the "shinin'" or the "sight." Ask someone who's been in combat if he ever had a feeling that he was going to get hit right before a firefight. You'll be amazed at the number of stories you'll hear about people hitting the deck a split second before a bullet whizzes through where they just were. Some people even hear voices that say "duck." You wouldn't believe the number of times criminals who got busted knew beforehand they shouldn't have gone to where they got popped. If you've got this gift, listen to it! It can and will save your ass!

There are other things to be considered when disappearing. One is conforming to shape. A shadow has a certain shape and flow of line. To disappear into a shadow, your body must conform to its shape and flow. If something sticks out, they're gonna know. When you hide behind a car or truck, make sure that your feet are behind the wheels. This is conforming to shape, as cars ain't got feet. The same thing when you're hiding in a toilet stall—get your feet off the floor! (Although it conforms to what people expect to see, I don't recommend you drop your drawers around your ankles, because if someone kicks the door open, you're in trouble.)

The human shape is easily identifiable for most people. Therefore, to disappear you must lose that shape. A human silhouette stands out; however, a dark lump is a dark lump. It is the head and the limbs that make the silhouette most recognizable. Lose those two defining marks and you just look like another lump. Curling up in a ball among a clump of shapes means you're just another item, not the person they're looking for.

The other option is to find something similarly shaped to hide next to. When I was a little bloke, some folks on horseback were searching for me during the night. A guy came riding up, and I was out in the middle of the road. I scooted over to the fence and stood perfectly still next to a post (we were sorta close in height at the time). The guy saw a fence post where it was supposed to be and not me. He rode within 4 feet of me. The horse was looking at me like, "What the hell are you doing?" But the guy missed me entirely. Legs snapped together to form a single line, shoulders hunched up around your neck to lose the neck shape, chest curled in with your hands on the front of your thighs to lose the shoulder taper, head down into your chest to lose the head silhouette, and to anyone looking straight on you're just part of a pylon, not a person.

Remember, people expect to see certain things, and if they see what they're expecting, they don't look further.

The other thing is *stay still*! I don't care if you have a Gila monster chewing on your dick, *freeze*! It's hard to see something that ain't moving! This includes taking shallow breaths to keep from moving your chest too much. If you go into soft focus, you'll see motion much more easily. Our peripheral vision is designed so that we can detect motion out of the sides of our eyes. If you freeze, though, all you have to worry about is the direct focus of your pursuers.

I know two guys who were legging it from the cops down in San Diego. They hit a ditch and hillside, and one splashed into the drainage ditch while the other shot up the hill. The cops showed up, and the one in the ditch slithered into an overhang. The guy on the hill sat down and curled up into a lump. The cops hit the guy on the hill with a search light and ordered him to come down.The guy in the ditch heard the conversation of the cops right over him. After the order to come down elicited no movement at all from the guy on the hill, it was repeated. The cop on the light was getting pissed that the guy upstairs wasn't coming down. After a bit, pissed turned into wonder. Around this time another cop showed up and said, "Man, that's just a piece of cardboard. Let's go." They got in their car and left.

The guy on the hill did the three things that I just mentioned: 1) he lost his silhouette; 2) he didn't look at the cops; and 3) he remained perfectly still, even when spotted. He didn't go to jail that night because he knew how to disappear.[5]

Now if you have to look at your pursuers (which again, I don't recommend), do it either from down low or way up. Down low is not where most people look to begin with, so that immediately reduces your chances of being seen. A head-sized object peeking around a corner at eye level is likely a person peeking around the corner (especially with the eye pattern). Something peeking around the corner near the ground could be anything (like a cat). More often than not, it will be dismissed outright, especially if you only peered around with one eye. Look at the ground and see how many lumps and bumps there are at ground level. Something low to the ground is easily over-looked (that's why cats crouch when stalking things). Peering at someone over the roof edge should only be done from the side. You twist around and only look over with one eye. As a person's peripheral vision will detect any flicker of movement, if what he sees con-forms to the familiar silhouette of a head and shoul-ders, you'll be recognized.

Okay, I'm going to go off into woo-woo land here for a minute for the final touch of disappearing. Ready, campers? Got your Twilight Zone bags packed? Here we go!

The last aspect of disappearing is the desire to dis-appear. This means you leave behind any emotional attachment to what is going on. You emotionally and energetically disappear from the place. If you're not there, there shouldn't be any emotions hanging around, should there? One of the reason the ninja could zippity-do-da out of someplace so well is they dropped into a mind-set that literally left them invisi-ble to the naked eye as well as the psychic eye.

If a group of people is hunting you, the hunters have a pretty good idea of what your electrochemical radiational field looked like when you jack-rabbited around the corner. (Like the way I said that?) When they come around the corner, even if you aren't in sight, they're still looking for that search image. If they're getting ready to go tearing down a certain way but there's a beacon over in the corner announcing, "FEAR! FEAR! FEAR!" somebody is going to throw a look over there. On the other hand, if there's a row of trash cans stating, "Normal background," they're going to ignore it. You can disappear by either blanketing any sign of your existence or taking on the shape of something else.

The same thing arises with hunting someone. If you approach someone as a hunter with "HUNT! HUNT! HUNT!" sirens blazing, you're going to alert the guy that you're moving on him (unless he's stoned, drunk, or seriously unaware). If, however, you're part of the background, he's not going to sense you until it's too late. Cops are real good at this disappearing trick, especially highway patrol. You get nailed and discover the guy's been right next to you, pacing you, for a while.

If you want more information as to what mind-set is needed to disappear, go hassle a ninja. I've shot my credibility to hell enough as it is.

Notes

1. I should also point out that this attitude, while functional (and accepted) on the street, will not make you popular with martial artists and bullheaded tough guys. People who are used to overpowering their opponents get real uptight with people who won't play their little game. Macho men rightly fear assassins.

2. That's how I disappeared at Tim's. I blended into a bump that was supposed to be there. They both saw the bump but wrote it off because it was normal. The eye will focus on a point, but everything else is sort of hazy and subject to mental shorthand. You can easily disappear between the points of focus. They were only searching the normal sleeping surfaces, not the entire area. They'd focus on something and haze out the rest of the room, and because of that, they didn't see me.

3. On the other hand, if you come to a three-way intersection and book down a way that doesn't leave proof of passage, their standing around with their thumbs up their asses wondering which way you went is going to give you time to escape successfully.

4. A LRRP friend of mine had an NVA soldier actually step on his outstretched hand. Talk about sphincter factor! He quietly did what I just said and split.

5. His clothes were also neutral colors, which I will talk about in the Boomtown section.

CHAPTER SEVEN

Big League Fox and Hound

> "When you're up to your ass in alligators, it ain't no time to be worrying about draining the swamp."
>
> —American provincial wisdom

There is a word for the situation I am about to describe, and that is UGLY! The situation is when you are on the hit list of a group. The reason this is such a cocksucker is that you never know when it is going to hit the fan. It's not like some sort of friendly fight where you can punch it out with someone and it's over. I'm talking about if they catch you, it's gonna be slow marching and loud singing for you. Now maybe there are still places where they'll just merrily beat you into a bloody pulp, but remember, I'm from L.A., and out here, they're gonna try to body bag you. This scenario is more extreme than what many people will find themselves in, so just take it and scale it back to whatever fits your particular needs.

Now you can find yourself in one of three separate situations where you are hunted: 1) a pack of amateurs are after you; 2) professional bad boys are after you; and 3) the cops are after you. In many ways, what you need to do is the same in all three cases, with only a matter of volume adjustment for each. In this chapter, I'm mostly going to deal with specifics applicable to categories 2 and 3. If you're not likely to have the Mafia or the police after you, feel free to skip to the next chapter. Or just read it anyway; it's kind of interesting reading, albeit a little technical.

There's some good news and some bad news here. If the cops are after you they have a higher likelihood of catching you than the crooks. That's the bad news. The good news is they're less likely to kill you than the crooks. You'll do some time somewhere and maybe get offed by one of the homeboys in the joint, but you'll be alive until that time. ("Good news" in this case is sort of a relative term.)

The main difference between being chased by the cops and being chased by the bad guys is that chasing and catching people is the cops' job. That means they're better at it than most of the bad guys. There's a reason more bad boys don't get taken down. One is a thing called burden of proof. The cops know who you are, where you are, and what you are up to if you're a player. They just don't have enough evidence to make a solid case. Unless there is a hot warrant on you, the cops aren't going to nail you until they really have something that'll stick. They may hang paper on you with small stuff, but that is to make sure they have all the information they need when they want to pick you up on the hairy stuff. Those so-called "scare cards" that cops fill out when they talk to you give them all sorts of ideas on where to look if you rabbit. Once or twice in the system and they know your network.

Two is there are just so many people out there the cops need to nail that they have to prioritize. Some small-time drug dealer is less important than a killer or a rapist. How bad the act was determines how hard the cops are going to look for someone.

If they really want to, cops can find you faster than bad guys can. That's because cops have these things called computers that can talk to other computers. It never ceases to amaze me the number of people who disappear yet still leave a paper trail. I love the guys who are on the lam but still show up at their mailing address on the first and fifteenth to pick up their state checks. All it takes is a phone call: "Yes, this is Detective So-and-So, is what's-his-nuts receiving unemployment? He is. Are you sending it to this address? Great, when does his check go out? Thank you!" The cops show up around the same time as the mailman and nab Mr. Slick.

Who's looking for you is a crucial determining factor in how seriously you have to disappear. If you've upset either the cops or the big boys, you need to effect a serious evaporation. I'm talking new identity and different state time. If you are running risky shit, the time to get your travel papers in order is before you need them. Depending on how serious your business is, you may need to drop anywhere from a few hundred to a few thousand dollars prep money and leave the system buried like a mole waiting to be activated. This is seriously heavy league, and it works against people who have resources and connections to hunt you. While your average gangbanger can't reach into another state's department of motor vehicles computer network, people with names like Luigi can. The other thing is, there are professional paper people who make ID. If you run to them during a shitstorm, you will discover they've heard the word about you already. You go see Joey the ID man and discover someone has already informed him that it would be in his best interest to talk if you show up on his doorstep. When you show up to pick up your new ID, there are a couple of torpedoes waiting for you. Ooopsie!

Both the heavy-duty bad guys and the cops know the most common ways people disappear. They also know something that most of these people don't realize: disappearing is harder than most people think it is. It's just a matter of patience; if they don't get their guy now, they'll get him later. (Usually because the guy ends up stepping on his own dick!)

First, did you know the Witness Relocation Program seldom works? Do you know why? Because people who have been living "The Life" can seldom adjust to everyday kind of lives. They're squirreled away in a different place with a new identity and a regular job in order to stay alive. Somewhere along the line, either the boss chews them out, they get bored, or they think they can get away with something, and they end up doing something that puts them back onto the circuit.

Contrary to popular belief, the circuit isn't that big. People are prone to seek out their own wherever they are. That means there are a lot of players scattered across this country who are actually operating in a small community. You can be in the same small community and be scattered over three states. Car thieves are going to know the chop shops in each city. A car thief from Philly passing through Arizona recognizes someone who pissed off the Philly family. Laughing boy is now working out of Arizona. A phone call later, and the guy who was "safely relocated" ends up with a bullet cavity in the back of his skull. Why? Because he couldn't stay away from The Life.

Animal's E & E Law Number 12: *If you have to seri-*

ously disappear, you do it all the way; halfway means caught or dead. That means you leave family, friends, possessions, and, most importantly, the way of life that got you into the shit in the first place. Like a basket-case alcoholic who has grabbed onto AA literally means it when he says "alcohol = death," going back to The Life = death. The number of bodies bear me out on this one here, folks. It's hard to walk away from The Life, but it's too small a world not to.

When you are being seriously hunted by either the cops or the big boys, they know that sooner or later most people will fuck up and surface again. That's why they aren't really concerned a lot of the time. They can be patient and wait. A warrant or a standing contract doesn't go away. In case you didn't know, the highway patrol in most states has the highest felony arrest record. Why? They pull some guy over for running a red light or expired tags and run his numbers through the computer. *Whamo!* Instant felony bust. That's where the cops stop, but in case you didn't know, it's real easy to get a hit put on someone in prison. If you get popped while the bad boys are looking for you, you're dead. Hell, if they don't have friends inside who will do you for free, there's always someone inside who will take a contract out on you. It's always nice to have $5,000 waiting for you when you're paroled out.

The truth of the matter is, if a professional wants you he's going to get you, bottom line. There are more ways to take someone out than most people would believe. Unlike with the woofers of the street, with pros there's little overt warning. The signs are real subtle that you've crossed a line, but they do exist. What is hardest for many people to accept is that in the big leagues you will probably get taken out by someone you know and trust. There's a shitload of bodies found with bullets in the back of the head that were

STREET E & E

whacked by someone the stiff trusted enough to let get behind him. The only way to avoid a professional hitter is to recognize when you have crossed the line and then ditch out with the network you've set up, as previously mentioned. Unfortunately, many people delude themselves into thinking that either it's a game or it would never happen to them. Consequently, they don't prepare for this likelihood and, as a result, they get an extra nostril blown in their foreheads.

Cops have only one thing to spend their time on, and that's catching bad guys. On the other hand, the bad guys gotta make a living. Drug dealers gotta deal drugs, bookies gotta book, gangbangers gotta bang, fish gotta swim, and birds gotta fly. That means in all likelihood their hunting you is going to be a part-time occupation. Past the initial piss-off, unless the guy hires a pro, chasing you is going to be a matter of convenience and opportunity. This is seriously good news, as it increases your chances of survival immensely if you're dealing with amateurs or people too poor to put a contract out on you.

By the way, how much money your hunters have will determine how good a hitter they'll be able to hire, especially if you split out of state. A pro will only take *you* out. They can do this with surgical precision. Those who can only afford a low-life or decide to do it themselves will usually end up with a sloppy mess. Sloppy means anyone near you also gets whacked. Friends, family, acquaintances, or even total strangers can get nailed in the cross fire for being around you. I once was talking to a guy who was boasting he had a contract on him. While everyone else was oohing and ahhing, I asked him how much money the people who were hunting him had. He looked at me and said, "Not much." I grabbed my chair and scooted it away from him. While everyone laughed, I wasn't really joking.[1] I get upset with yo-yos who think having someone hunting them is a badge of importance.

Let's look at a couple of things you can do to disappear that will make your life and your loved ones' lives easier, while at the same time making the lives of those after you harder:

1) The first pointer about staying out of the grips of your enemies: *no matter how tempting it is to run to mommy during times of trouble, do not go to your parents' house*. This—right after your girlfriend's house—is where everyone is going to look. If you've pissed off the psycho squad, you might have just set your folks up to have their house machine-gunned. If they are in it, hey, what can I say? Some of those bullet holes will be in your family.

Now here's something that, God knows why it happens, but it does. If you've successfully scrammed, *don't go home for the holidays!* Somehow, criminals figure the cops will expect them to come back for Christmas, so they think they'll pull a sneaky and come back for Thanksgiving. The cops have an early T-day dinner and then go round up the dumbfucks.

2) Number two, *avoid your normal haunts!* If you are a regular at Shady's Alibi Room, guess who's going to check to see if you've been around? A real fast way your hunters will use to get a friendly, well-meaning bartender or patron to tell them your location is the old "We've got some money for him" story. Especially if there's a tip in it—you can be sold out easily for $20. If someone is hunting for you, and he knows where you like to hang out, unless you really think you're bulletproof, you had better find a different place to hang out.

3) Helpful hint number three is *stay out of contact with old girlfriends and friends who might be pissed at you.*

Old girlfriends usually know who you're hanging out with these days, and if you're seeing someone else, she'll gladly tell whoever asks. You know that old phrase "Hell hath no fury . . ."? 'Nuff said.

4) Pointer number four is *CYA with the DMV, phone book, address directory*. If I got your license plate number for $4, I can get your address. Mail drops are good addresses to have on your license. Either chain your "home address" on your mail drops so they feed back to each other or to a trusted person's address. Out of habit you should have an unlisted phone number. If you don't, all someone has to do to find you is look in the white pages. The other thing is, except for police inquiries, you can put a phone company alert on anyone inquiring into your phone service. That way, if anyone calls up and inquires about you, a red flag goes up, and the phone company warns you.

There is a thing called the Reverse Address Directory published by the phone company. It is used by the 911 folks. The phone numbers are listed in order, with the addresses and owners afterward. If you have someone's phone number, you just go to the library and look up his address in this directory. If you request an unlisted number, make sure you request it in both directories. Unfortunately, this doesn't work against the cops, as they have a special phone number they call. Any phone and address in the system (listed or unlisted) is available to them. It's best to have a phone under an entirely unconnected name if you're really hot.

5) *If you are hiding out with a buddy, make sure his girlfriend isn't getting pissed.* A buddy will say, "Yeah, come on, I'll hide you." However, 99 times out of a hundred he forgot to check it out with his old lady first! She's going to get pissed at having your ass inter-

rupting her life because her old man feels some sort of obligation toward you. She's looking out for her own, and harboring a fugitive is a no-no. In case you're still thinking along the old neolithic lines of "A man's home is his castle," you're wrong! The home hearth has never been male territory. We are loved there (and sometimes tolerated), but do not think that women smile on having their home life interrupted by fugitives. A friend's wife will be the first to drop a dime on you (or let slip where you are) when you have overstayed your welcome. If you stay with someone, pay rent, utilities, and food expenses to stay in their good graces.

Another thing is don't do anything stupid while you're there. When someone is rabbiting from the cops, people get pissed if the person is still active, as that increases the chances of the cops showing up. In certain neighborhoods, if someone pounds on the door in the middle of the night, the residents know it's the cops (especially if the person staying there came blowing in an hour or so ago looking nervous). Your friend's old lady is not going to appreciate getting rousted out of bed in the middle of the night to deal with the cops because you couldn't keep from stepping on your dick. A lot of the time she'll say, "No he's not here," but when the cops ask to come in and look, she'll let them in! Guess who's about to get busted because you left her to clean up your mess? Somebody once said, "Freedom's just another word for leaving someone else to clean up the mess you made." Not in this case, bucko.

6) Rule number six: *you're going to need to do something about money.* If you run out and come trying to cage it off your friends and family, you're going to be in for a big surprise. Your hunters know that you're probably going to be coming back, and they will check

in now and then to see if you're around. Once good friends get pissed that you disappear then show up out of the blue and try to milk them, they are likely to let it be known to the wrong ears that you were around. Not only that, they aren't likely to give you any money. Who loans money to a ghost? If you disappear again, how are they going to get it back? Money loaned to a fugitive is money you can kiss off. I don't care how sincerely you beg him, a man with a contract on his head is not exactly a secure loan.

7) *Look out for snitches.* Especially when it comes to arrests, the guy who rolled over on you once before will probably do it again. If you've been popped before, that's one of the first places a cop will look to find where you are.

8) *Don't use your credit card or ATM card!* I cannot believe the number of people who run and then leave a paper trail a mile wide behind them. There is all sorts of interesting information that a skilled person can get by just looking at your credit card charges (legally accessible to the police and, for a small bribe, available to the bad boys). The cops want to know where you are, they just wait until you check into a hotel with your credit card. You leave a string of ATM withdrawals, and the cops know what city you're in. This is why the expertly prepared escape package costs so much; there are many more things other than a new identity involved, namely having established finances.

9) *Don't use a fucking car phone while you're running from the cops.* Back when I was running the correctional center, I had a big-time drug dealer get dropped in my lap. The DEA had gotten everything it needed on the guy by monitoring the car phone bands. Since it's broadcast, they don't need a warrant to listen in like

on regular phones! There you are on the run, and you say, "Yeah, Billy I'll be there in 10 minutes." Guess who else might be there waiting for you?

Running into a building isn't going to work, as most places only have two or three easily covered exits. If it's an office building, all they do is a floor-by-floor search for the guy who isn't in a suit. Same thing applies to an apartment building. The guy who's hiding in the laundry room is probably the guy they want. If you go into an apartment and take it over, that's kidnapping, and, next to murder, that's the worst rap you can get. You make whatever the cops have against you even worse if you do that. The other thing is, if you get a hostage, you also get SWAT. They're not likely to miss. So ixnay on the hostages.

Literally, the only way to get away from a helicopter is to dart into an indoor place where there are lots of people, like a mall. On the snowball's chance in hell that they didn't get your license plate number, this also works for your car. Get it into a mall parking structure and park it.[2]

If you can (like if it's hot), just walk away without parking it. However, if it's yours, see what you can do about parking it. It's unlikely that they don't have your plate numbers, but they might have missed. Then casually walk into the mall, wondering what all the excitement is about.

In either case (on foot or in automobile), once you're in the mall, first clean out your jacket pockets, then take it off and toss it. If you don't clean it out first, you're likely to pull something as slick as the bank robber who handed the teller the robbery note written on the back of his parole card. Or my stepdad's favorite, the guy they nailed when he dropped his wallet at the bank he'd robbed. They called him up and said they found his lost wallet, and when the asshole came in to claim it they busted him![3]

If you're just wearing a T-shirt, walk in and buy a different colored one and lose the old one. By changing your outer wear, you change your profile away from the guy they are looking for.

Oh yeah, important safety tip: if you've got friends with you, don't stay together and don't swap clothes; it won't help. You're still three guys wearing a red shirt, black jacket, and blue muscle shirt. There were two black guys who kidnapped and raped a woman in Marin County. They were in a bright red Cadillac in a 90-percent white county that only had five roads into it, two of which were toll bridges, where everyone had to slow down and cops could get a good look at who was in the car. When the cops nailed them they asked, "How'd you know it was us? We changed shirts!"

Notes

1. By the way, the group after him eventually caught up to him. It turned out they didn't have a contract on him, but they did take him down. They also took down a lot of people near the guy.

2. By the way, in case you haven't figured it out yet, it's best not to do anything illegal in a car registered to you or your friends. I knew a bank robber who borrowed his friend's car and robbed a bank. When the FBI showed up, the friend, who was totally innocent, said, "Hey man, he borrowed it that day." Thank you.

3. When he asked how they knew it was him they told him someone in line had IDed him. He was bummed out for a couple of days about someone rolling over on him.

CHAPTER EIGHT

Bush League Fox and Hound

"When your opponents are strong and outnumber you so you cannot be sure of prevailing, you should use humility to make them haughty, then wait for an opening that offers an opportunity of which you can take advantage and you can beat them."

—Liu Ji
Extraordinary Strategies of a Hundred Battles

The last chapter was pretty specific as to how to avoid getting nailed by the cops and big leaguers. It showed the most common mistakes that people pull while playing big-time tag. While it's interesting reading, it's not really much help if you're being pursued by the bush leaguers. Bush leaguers aren't likely to use computers to track you down. Remember earlier when I mentioned that there are three ways to get out of being hunted? Well, the previous chapter just covered the situations where the final option of declaring war doesn't apply. I also said there're three groups that can be hunting you: cops, pros, and bush leaguers. You cannot single-handedly launch a counter war against the cops or a professional group. If you hurt them they will come back at you and keep coming back until they get you, bottom line. It's safer to evaporate.

That's that, but what if you're stuck and you can't get out of there? You're being hunted by a bush league group who wants you hurt. I think at this time I should further divide the bush leagues into bush leaguers and total amateurs. While they will probably be offended by this, my opinion of youth gangs is that they are bush leaguers. Psychotic doesn't mean professional. I once had a gangster brag to me that there were more members of his contingent doing hard time than in any other group. I'm impressed. That proves they were experts at getting caught and convicted for long periods of time.

With the total amateurs, often all you have to do is wait a week and they'll pretty much forget about it. Either someone else will attract their attention, or they'll just blow it off. It's work hunting someone, and most amateurs are real lazy. If, after that time, you accidentally run into them, they'll be reminded that they're pissed at you and give chase, but they won't be hunting you actively on a daily basis. Kicking your ass will be a matter of convenience. These are the same guys who, if you hurt one of them during a pursuit, will blab to the cops that you did it. This is the pack of drunk shitkickers who think you've affronted the honor of one of their buddies and will spend a night cruising around looking for you. Once their honor is regained by this abortive attempt, they go back to being the slobs they are. Basically, all you have to do to survive these yah-hoos is lie low until they forget about it.

It's when the pack is serious that option number three comes into play. Generally, it'll take a week or so to get your counterstrategy organized anyway, and in this time you need to watch the heat level. If it has dropped off, you don't need to go to war status. If it keeps up, that's when you have to take counter-measures. Unless you're the invisible man, you can't run forever. If someone is after you on a serious level, it won't be forgotten after a few weeks. You have to go to war.

When you play tag with these guys, you have to remember that you are both the hunted and the hunter. In Robert Heinlein's book *Tunnel in the Sky*, the kid is advised when he goes on a survival drop to take just a knife rather than all sorts of heavy artillery. That way he will remember that he is the hunted, not the invincible hunter. Good advice, that. When people think they're invincible, they get cocky. When they get cocky, they get sloppy and make mistakes. This eventually formed itself into one of my opinions about guns. People think they're invincible when they're armed. Just because you're armed doesn't mean you can't be beaten to the draw! Always remember this and you won't make stupid macho mistakes that will kill you!

Animal's Law of E & E Number 13: *You cannot successfully do E&E if you have a John Wayne toe-to-toe-slug-out stupid case of macho.* You need to be able to ghost when necessary, attack from behind, and escape without delay when you are hunted. You must become a guerrilla fighter who knows when to attack and when to let your enemy exhaust himself on wild goose chases.

The first thing you need to do when it comes to this type of situation is always know your exits. Anytime you enter an area, figure out at least three different ways out of there. Go back to the back door and see if it opens. Also check what it opens into. *Mi hermano* Tim once walked up and checked the back door of a bar without looking to see what was out back. It opened and that was that, he thought. The shit hit the fan as it was prone to do in those days, and he was doing the "after-fight exit" when he discovered the back door led into a caged area where they kept the empty kegs. The cop who came to break it up walked over and tapped him on the shoulder and asked, "Would you like to come back inside?" Oops. That's a ha-ha funny now, years later, but it definitely wasn't funny at the time.

The reason you do this sort of strategic planning is you never know when the Glee Club is going to show up. Five hundred times nothing will happen, but it's 501 that you're thankful you planned for. If you haven't plotted this course out beforehand, you'll lose precious seconds figuring out where to go. In this situation, those seconds could spell the difference between life and death. Of course, if you know already that way leads to a dead end, you're not likely to make the mistake of trying to go that way, are you?

Also, when you are being hunted, avoid areas where there is only one way in and out. A cul de sac is a death trap. If you know about them, you'll know not to enter one in the first place—or to run into one when trying to escape. If someone sees you going into one of these places and he can get immediate backup, you're screwed. Even if they aren't there to kill you, they can still beat the shit out of you.

While sitting with your back to the wall should be standard operating procedure (SOP), when it comes to being hunted another variable comes into play. Don't sit next to the window. Someone driving by can look over and see your smiling face, especially at restaurants on the main drag. It's no problem to shoot through a window.

Now there is some debate on this next subject, location. Some people prefer sitting near the back door so they get a big head start on anyone coming in the front. I'm not one of those people. While most of the time a group of bush leaguers will all come busting through the front door, every now and then they have enough smarts to do what the pros do and send someone around to the back door. Some folks feel more comfortable tucked in a corner near the front door where they can get the drop on anyone coming through it. Some prefer the corners far away from all doors (I'm one of them), while others prefer being in the middle of a wall so they can watch both doors at once (which I'll settle for if someone's beaten me to the corner). In any case, these positions allow you to scan the entire area and who's coming in and out.

While it's okay to have a family of civilians behind you, you don't want too much room behind where you're sitting. Try for no more than two tables away from the wall to scan effectively. That's pretty much SOP as well, but it really comes into focus when you're being hunted.

The raw truth is, even though you're being hunted, life goes on. You have to make money, go to school, go to the job, whatever. It is this that will be your major problem with regard to being hunted. It gives you a pattern that makes you easy to find. Especially school. The only reason the Venice surfers and I clashed was we were both going to the same high school. If it hadn't been for that aquatics class, we'd have never even met.

Every day we knew the other side would be there. They knew we'd be together in that gym class. After I'd pulled a razor on them the first time, they knew not to fuck with me during class. However, it was on the way home that shit got interesting. Fortunately, we lived in different directions, so we seldom ran into each other. When we did, it got interesting, depending on who got the drop on whom. Once the common ground of school was removed, there was little chance of contact. I only ran into them that one time I got nailed.

Especially with the bush leaguers (and below), all
you have to do is stay out of their territory, and they're
happy to let the matter drop. When I was dancing
with the Venice boys, I stayed off the Boardwalk; that
was their haunt. I'll tell you the truth—those guys
would have let it drop a long time before if I had just
rolled over and paid homage to their grandness.
Unfortunately, I wasn't impressed with them, which
was how we got into the mess in the first place. Aside
from the casual maulings we'd give each other in
water polo, I have to admit a few retaliatory strikes
sort of kept the game afoot. They couldn't prove that it
was me who swung that trash can, but they were suspicious. Had I just ghosted (by dropping that class),
the whole thing probably would have blown over.

The issue here, however, was that we both had a
pattern that brought us together on a regular basis. If
everyone in the neighborhood shops at the same
supermarket, the odds are sooner or later you're going
to run into someone you don't want to see. These are
the kinds of patterns you must break in order to be
safe. Now, unless it's serious shit, I don't recommend
that you quit your job, but I do recommend that you
take a different way to work every day. Also park your
car away from the company parking lot, changing
location every day. Avoid set departure and arrival
times, although departure seems to be the preferred
time to strike. These are patterns that need to be
changed. If you're school bound, come lunch and
nutrition (or whatever they call the morning break
where you are), don't always hang out at the same
spot unless it's with a big group.

Perhaps the most important thing to do is *know the
escape routes* around where you're living and where
you must go regularly. If duty calls you to a place (or
it's near home base), figure out beforehand where the
best rabbit holes are. Depending on who's hunting

you, home can be a free base. One of the laws the Venice boys and I played by was that you don't nail someone in his home. If someone can reach his house, he's safe. Unfortunately, in some circles, not only is that not applicable, but they will machine gun your home—and everyone in it—just to get you.

In either case, you need to know the level of conflict you're involved in. If the free-base rule applies, knowing how to get to your home is most important. If the we-don't-care-how-many-innocents-we-take-out-with-you rule applies, you don't want to lead them to your home. Therefore, you need to have routes that will lead them away from your home.

Once these kind of players get ahold of your home location or that of your family members, you will get visited there. This is the most common trick of the L.A. gangs. They know the location of your parents, sisters, brothers, and anybody else you might hide with. Then they wait in a car down the block until they see you. When they drive by, they hose down the house. This is why there are so many "innocent" children hit by gunfire in L.A. The kid who catches a slug is the little brother/sister/ cousin/child of a gangbanger. The kid is innocent but had the bad luck to be related to a gangbanger. The other real common thing is the kid had the bad luck to live next to a house where a gangster hangs out.

By the way, if you're going to ghost out of a place and go stay somewhere else, *get the fuck out of the city!* Don't just move over to a nearby neighborhood. If you live in New York, go visit your aunt in New Hampshire. If you live in L.A. go see your cousin in San Francisco. Don't just scoot over 10 miles and expect to be safe (especially if you're going to still do the things that got you into trouble in the first place).

I once had a bozo who was stashed with me at the correctional center I was running for protection. He had offended the Shotgun Crips by ripping them off in a drug deal. (Not a bright move.) He had a female partner who tried to hide her own way. This guy—and God knows why it happens, but it does—had a sister who was a parole officer. The PO called in a few favors and got him stashed at my center. His sister was trying to get him transferred out of state, and he needed to stay low until that time. Well, the Glee Club caught up to his partner and left her splattered all over a front porch. Suddenly this guy went from big-time mouth to shaking rabbit. He was about to bolt when both his PO and I told him to stay low and shut up. He proudly explained to me that he knew the street and had people in Long Beach who could hide him. Against all advise, he zipped down to a place only few miles away from the Shotguns' hood. A few months later they found him and did decorative wall art with his brains. He should have waited and left the state.

Another thing to know is how likely your pursuers are to shoot. If they don't mind wasting anyone else to get to you, being in a crowd isn't going to help you. In fact, all that does is endanger your friends' lives and get them pissed at you. If group members are so stupid—excuse me, so bold—to walk up to you in the middle of a crowded place and pull the trigger, a crowd won't do you any good. On the other hand, pros will seldom move against you if you're surrounded by people. If they are going to murder you, even people you don't know will serve as witnesses. If you're dealing with amateurs who want to stomp you, they might not be shy about attacking you in public. Usually this is the case with teenagers, as older folks realize that there are all sorts of witnesses if they go after you in a crowd.

Animal's Law of E & E Number 14: *When you go deep, change your patterns.* If you are known to hit the track, don't do it anymore! If you like a good honky-tonk, you gotta change. Especially if the guys who are hunting you run along the same lines. I could avoid the surfers when not at school because we were into different circles. I wasn't likely to run into them, except at school. I didn't go to surfer parties, and I avoided "open" parties where I could accidently run into them.[1] Going to places where your enemies are likely to go is a great way to get your head blown off.

Earlier I said that there will be about a week's delay as you ready your counterattack. This time should be used to gauge how serious the guys are about looking for you. It also should be used as a period of recon and information gathering. The patterns that you need to change to be unpredictable are the exact patterns that you're going to use against them: where they are, when they're there, and what they're likely to do. To avoid an enemy, you need to know just as much information as you do if you are planning a counterattack!

Animal's Law of E & E Number 15: *Know thine enemy!* I'm talking names, addresses, car descriptions and license numbers, girlfriends, their addresses, family members, hangouts, schedules, normal activities, and also criminal activities. This especially means knowing points where they congregate and what paths they use to get back and forth. Believe it or not, most of E & E is not stumbling into your hunter's path. If you know that Joe Blow and his three buddies live up Washington Boulevard from the group's hangout, odds are that's how they travel between the two places. That's damn good incentive to keep off that stretch of Washington, isn't it? If three or four guys live in one area, you're more likely to run into that group in that area, aren't you? Where do they usually hang out, and where do they usually go to eat? When me and the boys were playing tag, I couldn't go to Gamboa's Gas House for lunch, as that was where they usually went to chow down off campus. What routes do members usually take for going from place to place? When are they likely to be on that route? Once you know the time and place of where someone is likely to be, it's real easy not to be there. That, more than anything, is the secret of street E & E.

Now let's talk about philosophy here for a second. Trip back up to the quote by Liu Ji at the beginning of this chapter. Liu Ji was writing a commentary on Sun Tzu's *The Art of War*.[2] If you decide that you have to go to war against your opponents, the week of avoiding them and gathering intelligence is going to make them overconfident and arrogant. They figure they've got you on the run. An overconfident enemy is a sloppy enemy.

The way to most effectively utilize this is to pick your targets carefully before you move. This is the time to remember the terrorist motto of "Kill one, terrorize a thousand." When you move, your targets are alone, and nobody is around to see what happened. In the early stages of counterwarfare, they can't know it's you! If they're still strong and they think that you're to blame, they're going to up the search. Since you have to operate normally during this time, the odds are that you'll get caught.

If you strike from behind, nobody is going to look your way until the guys who want you hurt have fallen down. Until they realize what's actually going on, you've ghosted as far as they're concerned, and that means you're not a threat. You are humble; they are arrogant. You keep them thinking that until it's too late. The shit I was into wasn't up to killing level, but a few people got nailed from behind with clubs and trash cans without ever seeing who did it. The reason I was able to operate was they were never sure it was me. They had other people who wanted a piece out of them, and they had to figure out who was responsible. It's possible that people will do something stupid and start shit with another group. People in a panic jump to conclusions. If a group isn't sure who's cutting into them they are likely to start shit with someone they think could be responsible. In the ensuing shitstorm, they're likely to forget all about little ol' you.

Another advantage to doing it this way is the group learns that they don't want to go off by themselves. When a group has fallen back to a solid defensive position, they're the ones who are locked down, not you. It's easier to avoid one big clot of your enemies than it is to have them ranging out by themselves. It only takes one guy to spot you and follow you for the word of where you are to get back to the group. On the other hand, if they're all sitting there with their thumbs up their asses looking over their shoulders, they're not going to be too effective about hunting you, are they?

Always remember, if they're looking for a psycho hunting them, they're not looking at a guy who, in their minds, ran away from them. That is someone they put low on the list of people to be concerned about. Now they might get the idea of rebuilding their confidence after it's over by picking on people they know they can beat, but if you stay low it's no real problem.

Now here's something I know we're all going to enjoy. You want to know the best way to disappear safely? Give your fan club something else to worry about. There is nothing like the cops coming down on someone to make him lose interest in chasing you. A car's license plate disappearing is going to mean Mr. Policeman will want to talk to these guys. If they're in a car with weapons out looking for you when they meet the minion of the law, well, well, well, isn't that too bad? A group that uses a car to cruise around looking for you is going to have a hard time if the car's engine freezes up because of an unexplained oil leak. An anonymous tip that so-and-so is carrying a piece on campus will take people out of the loop real quick.

Same thing with a Baggie slipped into a locker and a phone call.

It is actually incredibly easy to do this sort of stuff because people who are prone to chase others are often involved in things they shouldn't be. A video-tape mailed to the PD about your enemy's house being used as a drug-trafficking center will cause him all sorts of problems. Don't call the DEA if the guy is a petty dealer; keep it realistic and applicable, but call the heat down on him. If the guy has got a machine gun, tip-offs to the Bureau of Alcohol, Tobacco, and Firearms (BATF) really are a giggle. Use anonymous tips and videotapes as often as possible. Loads of laughs, let me tell you.

Cars are incredibly easy to sabotage, and a group that relies on one in particular is especially vulnerable to M&Ms in the gas tank, loosened lug nuts, disappearing oil that causes the engine to seize up, coated ping-pong balls in the gas tank (leaded gas vehicles only), etc. All will have the other team more interested in fixing the problem than chasing you. A little Baggie of drugs left under the driver's seat is always a real laugh, especially if the license plate has somehow fallen off.

Also, target people around them. An anonymous phone call tipping off the parents of the girlfriends of a group that they are involved in a dope smuggling ring will suddenly have the guys dancing to the heat they're getting from that direction. Married guys are real vulnerable to a female friend of yours calling his wife and acting like a drunk mistress who's pissed off that loverboy hasn't left the wife to run away with her. It's low, it's dirty, it's vile—it's also real effective and loads of laughs. Hit them from every possible side at once. The guy's old lady leaves him, his car blows up, he gets arrested, some other grunt is gunning for him for what he thinks Laughing Boy did, and his goldfish die. All of this happening at once will take his mind off little old you real quick.

In short, there are ways of making anyone's life miserable that are incredibly easy to do if you have a phone, a few simple hand tools, and someone's address. These things are designed to make the group's life pure hell, which keeps them too busy to chase after you.

Notes

1. By my junior year in high school I had pretty much left the teen scene. My social life was doing just fine, as I was hanging out with an older crowd and having a wild time there. Also, I knew I wasn't going to run into my li'l buddies there because those folks would haven eaten them for lunch.

2. A book I highly recommend—over Musashi Miyamoto's *Book of Five Rings* and hands down over Clausewitz' *On War*.

CHAPTER NINE

Making It in the Boomtown

"Keep your shit wired tight."

—The cardinal rule of survival in the Boomtown

I'd never been in a topless bar in Boulder, Colorado, before, and I was sort of looking forward to the experience. Rumor had it, this one was the best available in town. While supposedly there was a better place in Denver, we were in a borrowed car, and it probably wasn't the best thing to make the trip (not to mention the fact that the rickety old Toyota might not have made it all the way to Denver and back).

We blew into the large parking lot, and I swung the car around and parked far away from the door, pointed out toward the street. The guy I was with was more than a competent fighter; he was and still is a pro. He looked at me and asked, "Why we parking all the way out here?" There was only a single key on the fob, so I stuck it deep into my pocket. If there had been more than one, I would have figured out a way to leave the car key sticking out of my pocket while the rest were buried deep. As we walked across the parking lot, I ticked off my reasons for parking all the way out near the street the way I did.

"One, if we have to leave quickly, the car is pointed in the direction we have to go. Two, it'll give me time to get the key out as we run across the parking lot, and, three, I don't know this place."

The guy with me grunted and said, "Good thinking." I didn't mention issue four: I had just met him that week and wasn't too sure about his ability to keep out of trouble. For all I knew, walking into that place with him was setting me up for trouble. On the other hand, he's a smart cookie, and I figure he was thinking just about the same thing about me.

It turned out my fears were groundless, as I walked into one of the most mellow topless bars I've ever been in. After being in places where instead of a coat check you have a weapons check and you walk through a metal detector to get in, this place was as serious as playing patty cake. The girls had fewer tattoos and scars than I did; in fact, they were downright attractive. The interior decorator had opted against chicken wire anywhere. The bouncers were in tuxedo shirts and ties and spent most of their time with their backs to the crowd schmoozing with the cute bartender. Such was the quality of the one tough guy there that the cheerleaders in my old school could have kicked his ass. Yes, this was a mellow place. My precautions had been unnecessary, and it was an enjoyable evening.

On the other hand, when another buddy and I were out one night crawling through the topless bars of L.A., it was a different story. Being as when I have a few beers under my belt I'm a fearless fuck, we'd stopped in a dive in a neighborhood that definitely wasn't ours. For those of you who don't know, there's usually a pause between the time the music stops and when the crowd claps and makes noise that drowns out particular conversations. During this lull there's about a second or two of dead silence in the place. It was during that lull that my friend, who was trying to be heard over the blaring music, leaned over to me and, in a black topless bar, loudly exclaimed to everyone there, "I've never really found black women all that attractive." In light of the fact that we were two of the only three white faces in there, that probably wasn't the smartest comment I had ever heard.

I know this guy, and I know he's not racist. He had a mulatto girlfriend for five years. What he was that night was smashed and looking at something that was downright scary. The women in this dive were seriously tired. They *did* have more tattoos and scars than I do. In fact, the best-looking one there looked like she had been rode hard and put up wet. The rest of them went downhill quickly after that. What he had meant to do in his drunken haze was indicate his desire to leave this particular establishment, but a fluke of acoustics broadcast it to the entire bar.

Truth be told, had he actually said what he had meant, I think we would have died right there. Topless bar etiquette is when you're in there, you don't make disparaging comments about the girls. The quality of the girls usually reflects the quality of the clientele. While the girls were tired, the guys they were dancing for were even worse. Losers are usually touchy about the fact that they're the bottom of the barrel. Announcing that these guys were so low that the highest-quality woman they could get, even in the fantasy department, had a face that could stop a truck is a guaranteed fight. So maybe it's best that my partner sounded racist rather than condescending.

During the stunned silence that followed his announcement, I stared over my beer at the stage's edge for a second feeling every eye upon us. The girl on stage was glaring daggers at us.[1] I suddenly shot up to my feet and loudly said, "Right! We're out of here." I reached over and grabbed my friend by the collar of his jacket and dragged him up with me. I shoved him toward the back door and backed out behind him. The clientele watched me watch them watching us getting the hell out of there. This was enough to make them ponder the wisdom of following us, at least for a moment. They'd sized me up when we came in and, until that moment, had decided to play nice. Now they were considering an alternative.

When I got out the door, I hauled ass to the truck and jumped in. By the time my friend got into the truck, I had fired it up, and we were leaving. As we sped out of the parking lot three guys came out and stood by the back door to make sure we had done as promised. Had we still been in the parking lot, we would have been torn up. To this day, my buddy still doesn't realize how close we came to dying that night.

Those are two stories of having one's shit wired tight going into a situation. One turned out to be nothing, but the other could have turned ugly. The truth of the matter is you never know how the dice are going to fall and what will turn ugly and what won't. Therefore, you need to always plan for the shit hitting the fan.

A few books ago I introduced concepts called "the Boomtown" and "the borderlands."[2] The Boomtown can be any wild scene, while the borderlands are sort of the safety zones and/or crossroads between different life-styles. This is sort of a thumbnail breakdown, as often the two overlap so as to become indistinguishable. While violence can occur anywhere, it is in these two situations that it is most likely to occur. This last section consists of everyday precautions that you need to do to make it in the Boomtown and/or borderlands. These are things that come under the heading of keeping your shit wired tight with regard to E & E.

Incidentally, something that I've also mentioned before is closing the door to violence in your life. What that means in a practical sense is when you walk by some tough guys, give them as much attention as you'd give a lamp post. Yeah, sure, they're there, but you have to get to the theater in time to catch a movie; that's what's on your mind. A shitload of the time the toughs are wrapped up in their own stuff anyway and not noticing you. Other times they're just making a general broadcast as to their ferocity. At times like this, they're not really hunting, but if someone goes "EEEK!" in their general broadcast, they know they've found a victim. People who freak out that easy are high PEV (Personal Entertainment Value), and they will get fucked with. If, on the other hand, you just casually keep on going, you've not given them an opening to approach you. I'm not saying walk through their middle; in fact, steer clear of them as much as possible. Just don't quickstep and cast them "oh me, oh my" looks as you go by.

This doesn't mean ignore them. In fact, as you're going by you've dropped into soft focus (also explained in *Violence, Blunders, and Fractured Jaws*) and are watching for any movement from that direction. Once you're past them, remember what I said earlier about always checking six when you pass a group. If they decide to move on your approach, then you turn your entire attention on them. Sort of like a terminator targets something.

Scope them early, though, and you can avoid this problem altogether. If you see a group that looks too hungry, don't get close. Go another way, cross the street, go back to where you were, etc. So what if you have to get somewhere. Being late is better than being mugged, raped, robbed, stomped, or killed, isn't it? Think about it that way. Is being late worth any of those options? NOT!

I recently took some students of mine down to Hollywood. We spent the night wandering around the Boulevard looking at the flora and fauna, excuse me, the mold and the creatures. The trick, I explained, is knowing everyone on the street is one of the walking wounded. If you break it down, there are the cripples and the hunters. If you look at the strange-looking person approaching, you check which category he's in. If he falls into the cripple category, that means he's more interested in his own twisted shit than attacking you. It's when someone decides to bring it out that it's a problem for you. The good news is that there are varying levels in the hunter category. The percentage of cripple to hunter determines how good a hunter someone is going to be. Someone who is more cripple than hunter is going to be a lousy hunter and actually easy to handle. In fact, most people fall into this or the cripple category. They are merely opportunists; they won't move unless they see a serious opening. For instance, they aren't necessarily car thieves, but if someone leaves the key in the ignition, of course, they're going to steal it. In the case of attacking someone, if they see a quivering bowl of Jell-O, even they will make a move. Most of these people, however, unless they see a sure-fire opening, will not try to bother you.

On the other hand, a real shark is going to be more hunter than emotional cripple. This means he's able to go past his emotional limitations to become a serious threat. The absolute worst cases are the sociopaths and freaks. These are people who have parts missing. It's not that these parts are crippled; they're simply not there! It's either a blank spot or what *is* there you don't want to meet.

Now the *real* trick to determining the danger level is to figure out A) cripple or hunter. If he is a hunter, then B) is he actively hunting or just hanging out? Someone can be a hunter but not hunting. In which case, he's less of a threat. If someone is actively hunting, then you got a problem. At that point it becomes a matter of how competent that person is and whether or not he sees an opening. Unlike with an opportunist, the opening doesn't have to be big.

The reason I bring this up is, unless you have some sort of standard by which to judge what you're up against accurately, you're going to spend any time in the Boomtown starting at everything. That's no way to live. Once you install this search pattern into your mind you can quickly identify the threat level of people around you. A hunter who is more of a cripple is easy to shake off and convince that there are easier targets to go after. In fact, the purpose of this section is not only show you how to cover your ass regularly, but to give you a list of subtle little signs that you can send that will warn off the cripples with delusions of grandeur.

Perhaps the best way to look at general survival in the Boomtown is to remember a real simple point. Animal's Law of E & E Number 16: *In the Boomtown, you never know when the shit is going to go down, so always plan for it.* Truth be told, you never know when you're going to have to get the hell out of a place quick. Therefore, your standard operating procedure is to always arrange yourself in a position where you can bug out quick. Let's talk about a real basic one that people blow it with all the time—your car.

You will note that in Boulder I parked the car in a manner that would allow us to get the hell out of there in record time. Once we were out the door I'd drag the key out of my pocket as we were legging it across the lot. No lost time searching for the right key that would allow pursuers to catch us. By the time we reached the car the right key would be in my hand.

Also, there was distance involved, any pursuers weren't going to be able just jump on us right outside the door; they'd have to do some work and run across the lot. That's less appealing than being able to kick someone's ass immediately (namely because if you run to a fight you're going to be winded when you get there!). I don't remember who it was who said that the way to march a thousand miles and win a battle is to make the other side march it. The way I'd set it up, by the time someone caught up to us, they'd be huffing and puffing.

If you keep your car key on a ring with other keys, have something large that is identifiable by touch right next to the key. You need to be able to find your car key by feel. When you reach for the key ring you find the object that the car key is next to, that puts you in the right area to find it fast. Either have a different shaped key on the other side of the object, or put one of those rubber doo-hickies on your car key to make it identifiable by touch. All this reduces the job of finding your key at a dead run to a two-step process. When you're hauling ass across a parking lot with a group of people hot on your tail, you need this sort of streamlining.

The other nice thing about distance is it buys you time. Even if you have the right key, you have to slow down to get through the car door. If you park just outside the door while you're fumbling with your key at the car door, the guys take a few steps and BLAMO! They land on you. You can buy all sorts of time and distance by parking far out in the lot.

Another point is that the car is pointed in the

direction you wish to go. No backing out of a spot, stopping, and then going forward again. That loses you all sorts of time. If your fan club is shooting at you, the time it takes to accomplish that maneuver leaves you a sitting duck. Once I hit that ignition, we could have been out of there in a straight line and down the street. Bye! Bikers park their bikes front tire out for this same effect.

The car was not blocked in by someone in front of us. If you have to back into a space to achieve this it's all right. A more common trick is, on the street, always try to find parking spaces next to a driveway. You're less likely to get parked in. Being parked in means you lose time escaping. Lost time means they catch you and either fuck up your car, fuck you up, or arrest you. Not good. If you pull up into an open stretch of curb, move forward to that driveway. It's best to have your nose pointing into a driveway, but as a second choice, your trunk next to one is acceptable too. You may end up driving backwards for a while, but you're out of there PDQ.

Incidentally, another reason to park away from a place is to keep people from getting your license plate number. I can't tell you the number of people who have congratulated themselves on making a successful getaway right up to the moment that the cops knock on their doors. If you have people in hot pursuit, don't turn on your car lights until you're about halfway down the block.

I know I've said it before, but I'm going to say it again: *don't hang around a place after the shit goes down.* You may have won the fight, but it's time to get the hell out of there. Part of the reason I'm so intense on how to park your car is that if you don't do this, there is a good chance you may have to leave your car there. If they are in hot pursuit, you'll lose too much time getting your car if you didn't plan ahead. If there's folks on your tail, you can't afford any lost time.

Don't think it's just a matter of cruising back over to pick it up later, either. In smaller towns, or if the shit was seriously ugly, the cops will be hanging around. They will either close the place down or wait for closing. At this time, the parking lot clears out and the only car left is yours. Gee, could that be our man? If the guys know which car is yours, it's real simple to take the distributor cap with them or, if they're not that creative, just trash your car. Whatcha gonna do then? Oh, wait a minute, I forgot something. The civilized routine is to just tell the cops that's your car over there. (Sometimes I forget that there are civilized people out there.)

If you have to leave your car somewhere, it's going to take a phone call and a friend to get it back. If the goons have time, the parking lot is going to be watched; they're going to be waiting for your smiling face to come back. Your friend has to go and get your car. My preference is to use women for a pickup like this, as the goon squad is usually looking for a guy to pick up his car.

If there are cops watching, your friend has to come to the place and go in for a few minutes. Once inside, he or she hits the head for a minute or two and walks outside again. To an outside observer, it looks like the person just went in to get a car from someone inside. Since you're not in there, that's not who they're looking for. To the people inside, it just looked like that person had to pee. Unless they compare notes, nobody is the wiser. That is highly unlikely. As I mentioned earlier, people expect to see certain things. It's when they don't that they get suspicious. Someone coming to pick up a car from someone who's catching a ride home with someone else looks real normal. The wife who needs the car from someone in the bar also looks real familiar. On the other hand, someone just waltzing up to a parking lot and plucking a car out doesn't look normal.

Also it's better for your friend to walk a block than it is for you to drive him/her up to the front step. Incidentally, don't use your bestest buddy in the world for this, because if everyone knows you two are the Bobbsey twins they're going to realize what is going down when he shows up. Don't get anyone who looks like you to pick it up either. The cops have a vague description of you, and anyone who looks like you is going to be questioned. I can hear the conversation now: "No, it's not my car, it's my friend's car. Oh, you're looking for someone who abandoned a car here? My friend's name? Uh . . . George. You want to see the registration just to check?" They gotcha.

There are people more qualified to talk about evasive driving techniques than I. What I would like to point out to you is there is a difference between a tail and a hit. If someone is just following you, you can often shake him by stopping somewhere (especially by pulling into police stations). On the other hand, if he is coming to whack you, you don't want to stop. In case you haven't noticed, there aren't too many places to duck when you're sitting in a car. While people bitch about .38 slugs bouncing off cars, certain loads will punch through a car door like tissue paper. You don't want to stop and get out in these sorts of situations.

By the way, one thing you should know about, especially on freeways and turnpikes, is a thing called a "touch and go." I don't know what the highway patrol calls it, but it's what they do all the time to encourage silly people to speed. What it consists of is getting off the freeway and immediately getting back on again. A touch and go is also good for either establishing whether you are being followed or losing someone when you know you are being followed. If you think you are being followed, use full signals and get off. First off, if you're really being tailed, your escort will follow. At that point, it could still just be a coincidence. However, if they follow when you immediately get back on, they blow their cover and they know it. This works best on ramps that face each other across a street.

If you know you're being followed, you have to set it up so they cannot cross the lane to catch you. (This is not a pursuit trick, as someone who's coming to nail you won't care that you know he's there and will chase you anyway.) Without using signals, wait until the last second and then cut onto the off ramp. Other cars behind you make great shields to use. Large trucks both cut you off from the view of your tail and are too big to be buffaloed out of your pursuer's way.

Try not to make it so drastic as to be illegal, but wait long enough so anybody following you would have to break the law or do something dangerous to keep up with you. To any cops around, it looks like you spaced your off ramp and remembered just in time. That cuts down on your possibility of a ticket. If you get nailed by a cop, the odds are that whoever was tailing you is just going to innocently cruise on by. Try telling a cop that you were being followed and that's why you broke the law. He'll want to know what you've been up to to get followed in the first place. That line is more credible if a woman tells it, as follow-home rapes and robberies do happen. So unless you got boobs or your company's daily deposits with you, don't try that line.[3]

If you think for some reason that you're going to be involved in some sort of behavior that would entail high-speed chases, always inspect your routes before you go there for the real thing. Come a day early and look around for important things to know, like dead-end streets, areas with no outlets, road construction, possible ambush spots, etc. Also, come around the same time of day as the meeting will be so you have an idea of the traffic patterns. An area that's deserted around noon could be wall-to-wall traffic at rush hour.

Aside from the idea of having a fast car and taking professional driving lessons for E & E, you also might consider doing some modifications to your car. Most of the gang hits in L.A. are done from a stolen car. The car is dropped off elsewhere when it's all done. If you're not up to ripping off a car, I recommend some basic precautions. First off, never go anywhere with an easily identifiable car. There should be no primer patches, bashed in fenders, etc. Purple fuzzy dice on the mirror and bumper stickers are out too. "Find" some license plates that somehow gets on your car on the way to a meeting and fall off immediately afterward. As I've mentioned before, if I have your real license plate number, I can find where you live. So can anyone else.

There are all sorts of interesting things you can do with registrations, most of which are illegal but will keep people from finding you. On the other hand, having your car registered to a mail-drop address doesn't break the law per se, and it keeps you from having unwanted visitors. Using this system, when you meet Mr. Policeman, everything gels on your license and registration, and he stays happy.

Perhaps one of the more fun things you can do to your car if you're in a business where you regularly expect to end up in high-speed chases is a trick I learned from an English drug runner. Wire a toggle switch into your car's brake lights. It's easy to do next to your fuse box and loads of laughs. See, one of the problems of being chased in a car is that the people behind you know what you're doing because you're telling them with your brake lights. When you are coming up to a nasty curve and you hit your brakes, the guy behind you knows he should probably do the same. Without those pesky brake lights snitching on you you can apply all the brakes you want, while Laughing Boy behind you is still accelerating! Some cars are wired so you'll lose both your taillights and your brake lights, while others are on separate circuits. The latter are the best, because your pursuer is still seeing your taillights, but they both work.

Notes

1. She had taken it in the spirit it was meant and was ready to play show-and-tell with our genitals. Never tell a woman she's ugly, even if you're totally pissed. It ranks up there with using the "F" word on a woman for getting yourself torn another asshole. (Incidentally, the "F" word isn't fuck; it's fat.) Hell hath no fury, boys . . .

2. *Violence, Blunders, and Fractured Jaws: Advanced Awareness Techniques and Street Etiquette.*

3. Then again, if they are in full-scale pursuit, go ahead and do something illegal in front of a cop. Just make sure your pursuers do it too.

Conclusion

"All the world will be your enemy, Prince of a Thousand Enemies, and if they catch you, they will kill you. But first they must catch you."

—Richard Adams
Watership Downs

The quote at left is the one line that, to me, brings forth the thrill of the hunt. Unlike the rabbits that book is actually about, my feelings are "they must catch me before I catch them." If someone is going to hunt you, he has to accept that at any time he himself might become the prey. ("Don't gamble if you can't afford to lose, boys.")

When I have been hunted, I have never felt like a rabbit. I have, however, felt like a wolf chased by a pack of jackals. I can't take out the entire pack all at once, but one-on-one I can do serious damage. The trick, then, becomes to avoid them in force and catch them alone. That is not retreat; rather, it is a strategic withdrawal. I hope I have helped you understand that there is no dishonor in withdrawal.

The other point that I wish to convey is that sometimes it's just not worth the hassle to jam with someone just because he's not sure his penis measures up to the standards of manhood. If this kind of jerk doesn't see you, he can't pick you to prove anything on. While it should be a standard, it applies to too many things to make it an E & E law, but *if there's nothing to be won, don't waste your time fighting!* A mercenary tenet is, "Does the profit exceed the pain? If not, don't bother." A strategic withdrawal is a better course of action both in terms of ease and profit.

The term strategic withdrawal is more accurate than many would suppose. Not only are you not fighting someone on his terms, but you can often draw him into a situation advantageous to yourself. Lui Ji, a famous Chinese general, said, "Whenever you pursue people on the run, chasing beaten soldiers, you must make sure whether they are really fleeing or just feigning. If their signals are coordinated and their orders are carried out uniformly, even if they are running away in apparent confusion and chaos, they are not defeated. They surely have plans for surprise attacks, so you must take this into consideration."

The intent of this book is to either give you some idea of how to achieve an ordered withdrawal that will save you in crisis or show you how to draw your opponents into a trap. It's knowing how to avoid the traps and pitfalls out there that will save you if the cards don't fall your way. As you probably noticed by now, in life the cards don't always land in your favor, so it helps to have that option covered.

You know, there is much to be said about the evolution of a word or term. Many terms originally meant one thing but over the years have come to mean something entirely different. Such is, in my opinion, what happened to the term "martial arts." Sun Tzu was a martial artist. Genghis Khan and his generals Subatai and Jebei Noyon were martial artists. Napoleon was a martial artist. Gen. George Patton was a martial artist. Bruce Lee, however, was not. He (and thousands like him) was a specialist.

The literal translation of "martial art" is "the art of war." That's a mighty big topic that finer minds than you or I have pondered for more than a few millennia. The art of war is something that goes light years beyond just standing there pounding each other in a tournament ring. It means studying and understanding the myriad aspects of conflict and warfare, including the reality of how to retreat safely. To become a true martial artist, you must master all aspects of warfare, including when and how not to fight. Lao Tzu, in the *Tao Teh Ching,* said it best: "A good soldier is not violent. A good fighter is not angry. A good winner is not vengeful." This goes beyond the testosterone-crazed aggression and misplaced machismo we call "martial arts." It instead leads into something very special—professionalism. Very few American martial artists are professionals, and listening to them can get you killed.

I have in my office a poster of Murphy's Laws of Combat. My favorites are number 2, "If it's stupid but works, it isn't stupid," and number 27, "Tracers work both ways." But near the bottom is #32. It is rather simple, yet a profound statement that I'd like you to think about for a moment: "Professional soldiers are predictable, but the world is full of amateurs." I have to tell you that a number of things I have mentioned here will not work on real professionals, but the world is full of amateurs. If you go skittering over some rough turf, the pros will just look at it and say, "Another day." But the world is full of amateurs . . .

It is, however, the amateurs of this world that are

such a pain in the ass. A mafioso once summed it up perfectly when he said, "We don't kill people who don't deserve it." That's professional. If you're not playing their game, they pose no danger to you. On the other hand, the fucking amateurs are the ones who will make your life miserable just for the hell of it. Fortunately, they are the ones who think it's a game and will make aggressive, stupid mistakes. People who rely on testosterone and aggression will always fall before those who use cunning and flexibility. The old adage is true: "Youth and skill will always be over-come by old age and treachery." You don't get to be an old-timer by being a bozo.

You will notice that I used a lot of quotes in this book from Chinese sources. Face it, the Chinese civi-lization is the oldest existing on this planet. The calen-dar dates back about 5,000 years. The texts I have quoted here were written when Europeans were hid-ing in caves and barking at the moon. Egypt, Mesopotamia, Assyria, Hellenistic Greece, Macedonia, Rome . . . gone, history, kaput. China, it's still there. They've been around so long they don't bother to measure their history in kingdoms; they measure it in dynasties. Who was in charge that week. The S'hang, Xoung- nu, Mongols, Manchurians, they all came and had their heydays. Eventually, they fal-tered and died, but the Chinese endured. Communism is just another fad to these people, and it's following the same pattern as those others.

What's that bit of wisdom I heard from a Jamaican? "Trouble is like the tide, child, it come in, stay for a while, then go away. But it never gone forever, it alway come back and it alway go away again." It's the patient attitude that survives in the long run.

The Chinese understand that long-term survival isn't a matter of clashing head-on with every problem that comes along. Survival is a matter of knowing when to be hard and when to be soft. Against a gang, the only thing one man can do in a head-on conflict is get killed. On the other hand, one person who knows how to use hit-and-run tactics, utilize the environment, and use a group's weaknesses against it can turn from a ghost to a tiger then back to a ghost again. Someone like this can do much more than just get himself killed. He can survive the chaos of being hunted and can turn the game back on his hunters.

Sun Tzu said it all: "Be extremely subtle. Even to the point of formlessness. Be extremely mysterious. Even to the point of soundlessness. Thereby you can be the director of an opponent's fate."

Good hunting...

—Animal

Marc "Animal" MacYoung—Self-Portrait.

About the Author

Living all over the greater L.A. area, cultivating a warped sense of humor, and having a love of the 3 Bs (Booze, Balling, and Brawling) all landed Marc "Animal" MacYoung in more than his share of fights, scraps, jams, ADWs (Assault with a Deadly Weapon), and riots (seemed like a good idea at the time).

Discovering that, as a professional, he could get paid for his fighting abilities, he began a long career comprised of bouncing, body guarding, working event security, and running a correctional center, among other things (amazing what booze, extra strength, hormones, and a bad attitude can convince you is a good idea, isn't it?).

The good news is he's mellowed out . . . for him, that is. Now the bad news: Animal was recently witnessed roaring out of L.A. with his lady and cat. He was last seen in Barstow. Where he is now is anybody's guess. Sleep well . . . heh, heh, heh . . .